Derrida: A Very Short Introduction

Art Center College of Design
Library
1700 Lida Street
Pasadena, Calif. 91103

ART CENTER COLLEGE OF DESIGN
3 3220 00290 5417

VERY SHORT INTRODUCTIONS are for anyone wanting a stimulating and accessible way in to a new subject. They are written by experts, and have been published in more than 25 languages worldwide.

The series began in 1995, and now represents a wide variety of topics in history, philosophy, religion, science, and the humanities. The VSI Library now contains over 200 volumes—a Very Short Introduction to everything from ancient Egypt and Indian philosophy to conceptual art and cosmology—and will continue to grow to a library of around 300 titles.

Very Short Introductions available now:

ADVERTISING Winston Fletcher
AFRICAN HISTORY John Parker and Richard Rathbone
AGNOSTICISM Robin Le Poidevin
AMERICAN IMMIGRATION David A. Gerber
AMERICAN POLITICAL PARTIES AND ELECTIONS L. Sandy Maisel
THE AMERICAN PRESIDENCY Charles O. Jones
ANARCHISM Colin Ward
ANCIENT EGYPT Ian Shaw
ANCIENT PHILOSOPHY Julia Annas
ANCIENT WARFARE Harry Sidebottom
ANGLICANISM Mark Chapman
THE ANGLO-SAXON AGE John Blair
ANIMAL RIGHTS David DeGrazia
ANTISEMITISM Steven Beller
THE APOCRYPHAL GOSPELS Paul Foster
ARCHAEOLOGY Paul Bahn
ARCHITECTURE Andrew Ballantyne
ARISTOCRACY William Doyle
ARISTOTLE Jonathan Barnes
ART HISTORY Dana Arnold
ART THEORY Cynthia Freeland
ATHEISM Julian Baggini
AUGUSTINE Henry Chadwick
AUTISM Uta Frith
BARTHES Jonathan Culler
BEAUTY Roger Scruton
BESTSELLERS John Sutherland
THE BIBLE John Riches
BIBLICAL ARCHAEOLOGY Eric H. Cline
BIOGRAPHY Hermione Lee
THE BLUES Elijah Wald
THE BOOK OF MORMON Terryl Givens
THE BRAIN Michael O'Shea
BRITISH POLITICS Anthony Wright
BUDDHA Michael Carrithers
BUDDHISM Damien Keown
BUDDHIST ETHICS Damien Keown
CANCER Nicholas James
CAPITALISM James Fulcher
CATHOLICISM Gerald O'Collins
THE CELTS Barry Cunliffe
CHAOS Leonard Smith
CHOICE THEORY Michael Allingham
CHRISTIAN ART Beth Williamson
CHRISTIAN ETHICS D. Stephen Long
CHRISTIANITY Linda Woodhead
CITIZENSHIP Richard Bellamy
CLASSICAL MYTHOLOGY Helen Morales
CLASSICS Mary Beard and John Henderson
CLAUSEWITZ Michael Howard
THE COLD WAR Robert McMahon
COMMUNISM Leslie Holmes
CONSCIOUSNESS Susan Blackmore
CONTEMPORARY ART Julian Stallabrass
CONTINENTAL PHILOSOPHY Simon Critchley
COSMOLOGY Peter Coles
CRITICAL THEORY Stephen Bronner
THE CRUSADES Christopher Tyerman

CRYPTOGRAPHY Fred Piper and Sean Murphy
DADA AND SURREALISM David Hopkins
DARWIN Jonathan Howard
THE DEAD SEA SCROLLS Timothy Lim
DEMOCRACY Bernard Crick
DERRIDA Simon Glendinning
DESCARTES Tom Sorell
DESERTS Nick Middleton
DESIGN John Heskett
DINOSAURS David Norman
DIPLOMACY Joseph M. Siracusa
DOCUMENTARY FILM Patricia Aufderheide
DREAMING J. Allan Hobson
DRUGS Leslie Iversen
DRUIDS Barry Cunliffe
EARLY MUSIC Thomas Kelly
THE EARTH Martin Redfern
ECONOMICS Partha Dasgupta
EGYPTIAN MYTH Geraldine Pinch
EIGHTEENTH-CENTURY BRITAIN Paul Langford
THE ELEMENTS Philip Ball
EMOTION Dylan Evans
EMPIRE Stephen Howe
ENGELS Terrell Carver
ENGLISH LITERATURE Jonathan Bate
EPIDEMIOLOGY Roldolfo Saracci
ETHICS Simon Blackburn
THE EUROPEAN UNION John Pinder and Simon Usherwood
EVOLUTION Brian and Deborah Charlesworth
EXISTENTIALISM Thomas Flynn
FASCISM Kevin Passmore
FASHION Rebecca Arnold
FEMINISM Margaret Walters
FILM MUSIC Kathryn Kalinak
THE FIRST WORLD WAR Michael Howard
FOLK MUSIC Mark Slobin
FORENSIC PSYCHOLOGY David Canter
FORENSIC SCIENCE Jim Fraser
FOSSILS Keith Thomson
FOUCAULT Gary Gutting
FREE SPEECH Nigel Warburton
FREE WILL Thomas Pink
FRENCH LITERATURE John D. Lyons
THE FRENCH REVOLUTION William Doyle
FREUD Anthony Storr
FUNDAMENTALISM Malise Ruthven
GALAXIES John Gribbin
GALILEO Stillman Drake
GAME THEORY Ken Binmore
GANDHI Bhikhu Parekh
GENIUS Andrew Robinson
GEOGRAPHY John Matthews and David Herbert
GEOPOLITICS Klaus Dodds
GERMAN LITERATURE Nicholas Boyle
GERMAN PHILOSOPHY Andrew Bowie
GLOBAL CATASTROPHES Bill McGuire
GLOBAL WARMING Mark Maslin
GLOBALIZATION Manfred Steger
THE GREAT DEPRESSION AND THE NEW DEAL Eric Rauchway
HABERMAS James Gordon Finlayson
HEGEL Peter Singer
HEIDEGGER Michael Inwood
HERODOTUS Jennifer T. Roberts
HIEROGLYPHS Penelope Wilson
HINDUISM Kim Knott
HISTORY John H. Arnold
THE HISTORY OF ASTRONOMY Michael Hoskin
THE HISTORY OF LIFE Michael Benton
THE HISTORY OF MEDICINE William Bynum
THE HISTORY OF TIME Leofranc Holford-Strevens
HIV/AIDS Alan Whiteside
HOBBES Richard Tuck
HUMAN EVOLUTION Bernard Wood
HUMAN RIGHTS Andrew Clapham
HUMANISM Stephen Law
HUME A. J. Ayer
IDEOLOGY Michael Freeden
INDIAN PHILOSOPHY Sue Hamilton
INFORMATION Luciano Floridi
INNOVATION Mark Dodgson and David Gann
INTELLIGENCE Ian J. Deary
INTERNATIONAL MIGRATION Khalid Koser
INTERNATIONAL RELATIONS Paul Wilkinson
ISLAM Malise Ruthven
ISLAMIC HISTORY Adam Silverstein

JOURNALISM Ian Hargreaves
JUDAISM Norman Solomon
JUNG Anthony Stevens
KABBALAH Joseph Dan
KAFKA Ritchie Robertson
KANT Roger Scruton
KEYNES Robert Skidelsky
KIERKEGAARD Patrick Gardiner
THE KORAN Michael Cook
LANDSCAPES AND GEOMORPHOLOGY Andrew Goudie and Heather Viles
LATE ANTIQUITY Gillian Clark
LAW Raymond Wacks
THE LAWS OF THERMODYNAMICS Peter Atkins
LEADERSHIP Keith Grint
LINCOLN Allen C. Guelzo
LINGUISTICS Peter Matthews
LITERARY THEORY Jonathan Culler
LOCKE John Dunn
LOGIC Graham Priest
MACHIAVELLI Quentin Skinner
THE MARQUIS DE SADE John Phillips
MARTIN LUTHER Scott H. Hendrix
MARX Peter Singer
MATHEMATICS Timothy Gowers
THE MEANING OF LIFE Terry Eagleton
MEDICAL ETHICS Tony Hope
MEDIEVAL BRITAIN John Gillingham and Ralph A. Griffiths
MEMORY Jonathan K. Foster
MICHAEL FARADAY Frank A. J. L. James
MODERN ART David Cottington
MODERN CHINA Rana Mitter
MODERN IRELAND Senia Pašeta
MODERN JAPAN Christopher Goto-Jones
MODERNISM Christopher Butler
MOLECULES Philip Ball
MORMONISM Richard Lyman Bushman
MUHAMMAD Jonathan A. C. Brown
MUSIC Nicholas Cook
MYTH Robert A. Segal
NATIONALISM Steven Grosby
NELSON MANDELA Elleke Boehmer
NEOLIBERALISM Manfred Steger and Ravi Roy
THE NEW TESTAMENT Luke Timothy Johnson
THE NEW TESTAMENT AS LITERATURE Kyle Keefer
NEWTON Robert Iliffe
NIETZSCHE Michael Tanner
NINETEENTH-CENTURY BRITAIN Christopher Harvie and H. C. G. Matthew
THE NORMAN CONQUEST George Garnett
NORTH AMERICAN INDIANS Theda Perdue and Michael D. Green
NORTHERN IRELAND Marc Mulholland
NOTHING Frank Close
NUCLEAR POWER Maxwell Irvine
NUCLEAR WEAPONS Joseph M. Siracusa
NUMBERS Peter M. Higgins
THE OLD TESTAMENT Michael D. Coogan
ORGANIZATIONS Mary Jo Hatch
PAGANISM Owen Davies
PARTICLE PHYSICS Frank Close
PAUL E. P. Sanders
PENTECOSTALISM William K. Kay
PHILOSOPHY Edward Craig
PHILOSOPHY OF LAW Raymond Wacks
PHILOSOPHY OF SCIENCE Samir Okasha
PHOTOGRAPHY Steve Edwards
PLANETS David A. Rothery
PLATO Julia Annas
POLITICAL PHILOSOPHY David Miller
POLITICS Kenneth Minogue
POSTCOLONIALISM Robert Young
POSTMODERNISM Christopher Butler
POSTSTRUCTURALISM Catherine Belsey
PREHISTORY Chris Gosden
PRESOCRATIC PHILOSOPHY Catherine Osborne
PRIVACY Raymond Wacks
PROGRESSIVISM Walter Nugent
PROTESTANTISM Mark A. Noll
PSYCHIATRY Tom Burns
PSYCHOLOGY Gillian Butler and Freda McManus
PURITANISM Francis J. Bremer
THE QUAKERS Pink Dandelion

QUANTUM THEORY John Polkinghorne
RACISM Ali Rattansi
THE REAGAN REVOLUTION Gil Troy
THE REFORMATION Peter Marshall
RELATIVITY Russell Stannard
RELIGION IN AMERICA Timothy Beal
THE RENAISSANCE Jerry Brotton
RENAISSANCE ART
Geraldine A. Johnson
RISK Baruch Fischhoff and John Kadvany
ROMAN BRITAIN Peter Salway
THE ROMAN EMPIRE Christopher Kelly
ROMANTICISM Michael Ferber
ROUSSEAU Robert Wokler
RUSSELL A. C. Grayling
RUSSIAN LITERATURE Catriona Kelly
THE RUSSIAN REVOLUTION
S. A. Smith
SCHIZOPHRENIA
Chris Frith and Eve Johnstone
SCHOPENHAUER Christopher Janaway
SCIENCE AND RELIGION
Thomas Dixon
SCIENCE FICTION David Seed
THE SCIENTIFIC REVOLUTION
Lawrence M. Principe
SCOTLAND Rab Houston
SEXUALITY Véronique Mottier
SHAKESPEARE Germaine Greer
SIKHISM Eleanor Nesbitt
SOCIAL AND CULTURAL
ANTHROPOLOGY
John Monaghan and Peter Just
SOCIALISM Michael Newman
SOCIOLOGY Steve Bruce
SOCRATES C. C. W. Taylor
THE SOVIET UNION Stephen Lovell
THE SPANISH CIVIL WAR
Helen Graham
SPANISH LITERATURE Jo Labanyi
SPINOZA Roger Scruton
STATISTICS David J. Hand
STUART BRITAIN John Morrill
SUPERCONDUCTIVITY
Stephen Blundell
TERRORISM Charles Townshend
THEOLOGY David F. Ford
THOMAS AQUINAS Fergus Kerr
TOCQUEVILLE Harvey C. Mansfield
TRAGEDY Adrian Poole
THE TUDORS John Guy
TWENTIETH-CENTURY
BRITAIN Kenneth O. Morgan
THE UNITED NATIONS
Jussi M. Hanhimäki
THE U.S. CONGRESS Donald A. Ritchie
UTOPIANISM Lyman Tower Sargent
THE VIKINGS Julian Richards
VIRUSES Dorothy H. Crawford
WITCHCRAFT Malcolm Gaskill
WITTGENSTEIN A. C. Grayling
WORLD MUSIC Philip Bohlman
THE WORLD TRADE
ORGANIZATION Amrita Narlikar
WRITING AND SCRIPT
Andrew Robinson

Available soon:

DICTIONARIES
Lynda Mugglestone
DEVELOPMENTAL BIOLOGY
Lewis Wolpert
MADNESS Andrew Scull
MULTICULTURALISM Ali Rattansi
ENVIRONMENTAL ECONOMICS
Stephen Smith

For more information visit our website
www.oup.com/vsi/

194
D438
G558
2011

Simon Glendinning

DERRIDA

A Very Short Introduction

Art Center College of Design
Library
1700 Lida Street
Pasadena, Calif. 91103

OXFORD
UNIVERSITY PRESS

Great Clarendon Street, Oxford OX2 6DP

Oxford University Press is a department of the University of Oxford.
It furthers the University's objective of excellence in research, scholarship,
and education by publishing worldwide in

Oxford New York

Auckland Cape Town Dar es Salaam Hong Kong Karachi
Kuala Lumpur Madrid Melbourne Mexico City Nairobi
New Delhi Shanghai Taipei Toronto

With offices in

Argentina Austria Brazil Chile Czech Republic France Greece
Guatemala Hungary Italy Japan Poland Portugal Singapore
South Korea Switzerland Thailand Turkey Ukraine Vietnam

Oxford is a registered trade mark of Oxford University Press
in the UK and in certain other countries

Published in the United States
by Oxford University Press Inc., New York

© Simon Glendinning 2011

The moral rights of the author have been asserted
Database right Oxford University Press (maker)

First published 2011

All rights reserved. No part of this publication may be reproduced,
stored in a retrieval system, or transmitted, in any form or by any means,
without the prior permission in writing of Oxford University Press,
or as expressly permitted by law, or under terms agreed with the appropriate
reprographics rights organization. Enquiries concerning reproduction
outside the scope of the above should be sent to the Rights Department,
Oxford University Press, at the address above

You must not circulate this book in any other binding or cover
and you must impose the same condition on any acquirer

British Library Cataloguing in Publication Data
Data available

Library of Congress Cataloging in Publication Data
Data available

Typeset by SPI Publisher Services, Pondicherry, India
Printed in Great Britain by
Ashford Colour Press Ltd, Gosport, Hampshire

ISBN: 978-0-19-280345-0

1 3 5 7 9 10 8 6 4 2

To Geoffrey and the angels

Contents

Acknowledgements

Art Center College of Design
Library
1700 Lida Street
Pasadena, Calif. 91103

I would not have found a way to write this book at all without the patience and encouragement of my students in the European Institute at the London School of Economics and Political Science. Many of them do not have a background in philosophy, and Derrida is almost invariably a known unknown. The courage they show stepping into such uncharted waters makes teaching a perfect pleasure, and I would like to thank them for their enthusiastic participation, their interest – and their ideas.

Various people whose scholarship on Derrida I admire enormously have read or heard drafts of parts of this text as lectures or seminars, and I am particularly grateful to Geoffrey Bennington, John Cottingham, Robert Eaglestone, Marian Hobson, Peggy Kamuf, Oisín Keohane, Stephen Mulhall, Antonia Pont, Jack Reynolds, Nicholas Royle, and Henry Staten for comments and discussions. I would also like to thank the publisher's readers who read the first draft, and saved me from numerous errors and misunderstandings.

Finally, I would like to thank two of the editors at Oxford University Press, Emma Marchant and Peter Momtchiloff, who guided this ship home when, really, it could have gone anywhere.

Simon Glendinning
London, 2011

Chapter 1
A picture of Derrida

> Who is more faithful to reason's call, who hears it with a keener ear . . . the one who offers questions in return and tries to think through the possibility of that summons, or the one who does not want to hear any question about the reason of reason?
>
> Jacques Derrida

Jacques Derrida, father of the philosophical movement of deconstruction, was born at his family's holiday home in the small but busy town of El-Biar, near Algiers, Algeria, in . . . but wait, hang on.

We can come back to that conventional starting point in the life of the philosopher, that starting point without which nothing would have taken place at all. But the philosopher we are concerned with in this book wanted us to get on without paying much attention to that kind of starting point, without paying that kind of attention to the figure of the author, the supposedly creative origin behind the work.

One might find it ironic that a thinker so cautious about the appeal to a proper name, and 'the real life of these existences "of flesh and bone"' spent most of his days devoted to reading and discussing work by very singular figures within, especially, the history of philosophy: Plato, Aristotle, St Augustine, Montaigne,

Descartes, Leibniz, Rousseau, Kant, Hegel, Nietzsche, Marx, Husserl, Heidegger, Levinas, and many more. 'So-and-so's text' is one of the most common points of departure and springboards for his thinking. Some have thought that this is characteristic of a more general trend in philosophy: what has been called 'Continental philosophy' is often described as concerned primarily with proper names, in contrast to analytic philosophy's interest in problems. However, one would not have to dig very far into 'Derrida's text' to find such a construal called into question. For example, in one of Derrida's early and most important books, *Of Grammatology*, he insists that 'the indicative value' that he attributes to 'the names of authors' or the 'doctrines' associated with those names (Platonism, Cartesianism, Rousseauism, and so on) is 'the name of a problem'. The problem here is that it is naive to think of the author's names as designating *either* an 'origin' or 'cause' of the historical displacements and structures that are visible within the history of metaphysics *or* as 'simple *effects* of structure'. And the difficulty is multiplied because the texts he wants to read from the history of philosophy are themselves elaborated within the premises of this naivety. The idea of a contrast between the agency of great authors and movements, on the one hand, and determining historical structures, on the other, belongs at the heart of the metaphysics that he wants to question.

We will see later on how Derrida attempts to find a way of dealing with this problem, or at least of effectively working, albeit provisionally, with the conceptuality he is also questioning. For the moment, I just want to highlight a certain caution within 'Derrida's text' expressed towards any simple way of thinking through what we are to understand by that phrase, and that part of the non-simplicity here concerns the status of the author as the creative origin of a text or movement or historical formation.

Not that we can or should abandon such a concept. It is not as if we have another that might be more fitting. So practising this caution effectively has to negotiate with naivety. We have to accept saying that, for example, Jacques Derrida is the father of the philosophical movement of deconstruction and was born at a certain time and in a certain place. But we must also be ready to let 'Derrida's text' teach us that we should not rely too naively on the concepts through which we habitually understand such apparently simple sayings.

In short, any effort to engage with the biography of Jacques Derrida would have to take into account that the person whose life is the object of its study had a lot to say about the biographical genre, and, in fact, regularly insisted that, especially with respect to the lives of philosophers, there is very little value in the idea of seeking an accounting of 'so-and-so's text' by thinking one can simply refer to what went on in 'the real life of these existences "of flesh and bone"'.

Of course, Jacques Derrida did have flesh and bone. If you never saw him in person you can still see lots of photographs of him online, and there is a very fine portrait of him at the end of this chapter that I will come back to. Supposing that you now take the opportunity to look at some of these photographs, then you will, in each case, be looking at an image – a captured visual record of a now-past 'now' in someone's life – of a person who is now actually dead (and I can be sure of this whatever 'now' it is for you now). Although images like these can, nowadays, be created and sent almost instantaneously, the moment of delay necessarily involved, however brief, is always long enough to make it so that the *possibility* of such an actuality – the possibility that you are looking at a photograph of a now *actually* dead person – belongs to every photograph of a person that will ever be taken. This possibility will also always be an opportunity for a certain species of literary pathos. The philosopher Cora Diamond brings this out in her reflections on Ted Hughes's poem 'Six Young Men':

> The speaker in the poem looks at a photo of six smiling young men, seated in a familiar spot . . . The men are profoundly, fully alive,

> one bashfully lowering his eyes, one chewing a piece of grass, one is 'ridiculous with cocky pride'. Within six months of the picture having being taken all six were dead.

Another philosopher, John McDowell, countered that the 'sense of dislocation' that Diamond evokes with this description did not require the sudden interruption of young life and, indeed, 'could have been voiced if the young men had died peacefully after long and fulfilling lives'. I think Derrida would want to add to this that such a sense of dislocation does not even have to wait for their actual death. The *possibility* of a person's death, the possibility that I might be sure, from now on, for every now on, that you are looking at a picture of a dead person, the possibility of the 'absolutely gone' of a flesh-and-bone existence, haunts the picture, haunts the photograph, haunts every captured moment of a life.

So we have a worry with a naive emphasis on the author figure, as the creative origin of a work. We have, in addition, what one might call the 'death effect' of a photograph of a living thing or person. Jacques Derrida, the man captured in middle age in the photo at the end of this chapter, took both of these worries very seriously. However, one thing you might find it harder to read in photographs of this man, a third issue we might bring up around photographs of the author figure Jacques Derrida, is that he was personally uncomfortable with his looks, and so didn't much like seeing pictures of himself. This anxiety is perhaps harder to fathom since, as the photographs pretty clearly show, Jacques Derrida was a very good-looking man, at least an unusually good-looking philosopher. And he dressed well too: crisp shirts and well-cut suits. With his lively brown eyes and dark skin accentuating a shock of silver-white hair, Jacques Derrida stood out in the crowds in which he moved.

Perhaps aware of his good looks, but not happy to be thus aware, the philosopher Jacques Derrida was not at ease with the way he looked. He would speak of a 'narcissistic horror'.

You might find it interesting and helpful to watch a short interview with Jacques Derrida in which he talks about this horror and the other issues around photographs of Jacques Derrida that I have just introduced. It is on YouTube at http://www.youtube.com/watch?v=4RjLOxrloJ0

The conversation begins with the interviewer noting that until 1979, some ten years after he had achieved considerable fame as the Algerian-born father of deconstruction, Jacques Derrida 'had been very strict with the distribution of [his] image'. Jacques Derrida goes on to say that until 1969, and so before he was really famous, he had completely forbidden all public photographs of himself, in any form, from appearing. He gives his reasons – the reasons I have just run through – characteristically forcefully. He notes first of all that his own work called for the 'defetishization' of the author figure, and that he opposed the contemporary trend of using a 'head-shot' picture of the author in book publicity. For Derrida, as we shall see, a kind of withdrawal, a sort of solitude, is the proper mark of the expression of the one who appears, in a different way, *in their writing*. Jacques Derrida would have liked to have kept things that way. But his growing number of appearances at academic conferences and other public events made it impossible to prevent publication of photographs. His engagements were too public, his writings too well known. He could not control it. And so slowly he let it go. Whether he liked it or not, pictures appeared anyway, and eventually he consented to be photographed. One of the many published photographs of Derrida, one that was used on the back cover of his book *The Truth in Painting*, has been reproduced at the end of this chapter. Take a look at it. I remember seeing that picture while browsing in a bookshop. Seen alongside jacket pictures of other philosophers, the author of this book, the Algerian-born father of deconstruction, Jacques Derrida, looked, well, forgive me, he looked *really* cool.

In the interview, Derrida states that the theoretical (but also social and political) reason for wanting to avoid the ubiquitous use of author head-shots was not the only motivation for not releasing photographs of himself. And then the two further reasons are adduced: his discomfort and anxiety about undergoing the experience of seeing the image of his own good-looking face ('I don't like seeing it. I don't like it.'), and, in addition, 'the death effect' implied in every picture. But in later life, he found that there could be 'something good' too, 'in allowing other people to take what they want'. So that is where we are up to. The man in the picture had learned to let it go. He had learned that he could not control what he made public, and he learned to let go.

Jacques Derrida, father of the philosophical movement of deconstruction, was born at his family's holiday home in the small but busy town of El-Biar, near Algiers, Algeria, on 15 July 1930 to Sephardic Jewish parents. He was named Jackie Derrida, after the actor Jackie Coogan, by his American-film-loving parents. Only when he wanted to cultivate a more serious academic profile did he replace Jackie with the more formal, and French, Jacques. As a young man, he excelled at sport and in his teens he aspired to be a professional footballer. However, by the time he was eighteen he was influenced by Jean-Paul Sartre's role as an intellectual activist, 'a model' he later said 'that I have since judged to be ill-fated and catastrophic, but one I still love. . . '. At this time, Derrida dreamt of teaching and writing literature. But it was philosophy that formed the centre of his studies when he became a boarding student at the Lycée Louis-le-Grand in Paris in his early twenties, and it was philosophy, in one way or another, that came to dominate the rest of his life. He gave his first academic paper to a conference in 1959 and took a teaching post at the Lycée in Le Mans. Despite suffering acute depression at the end of the school year, he managed to get work teaching 'general philosophy of logic' at the Sorbonne while doing research on phenomenology and structuralism. Finally a successful academic career became a realistic hope, and 1967 was his breakthrough year, with three major publications: *Speech and Phenomena* (on Husserl), *Writing and Difference* (a collection of essays), and *Of Grammatology*

Jacques Derrida © Julio Donoso/Sygma/Corbia

(a masterpiece). By 1994, he had become widely regarded as the foremost thinker of his age – indeed, the age itself could be said to have become the age of deconstruction. He died of pancreatic cancer in hospital in Paris on the evening of 8 October 2004. He was 74 years old.

He was loved. He was also reviled, hated, smeared.

Chapter 2
Misunderestimating Derrida

Cambridge

It is hard to describe, let alone explain, quite how violently hostile the reaction to Derrida was, especially in philosophy, or why his work found an equally intense but positive reaction among others in the arts and humanities. But there are reasons for it. First, there is the vertiginous prose style, spinning itself out in multiple directions and at different speeds in ways that challenge even the most generous and well-prepared readers. 'Derrida's text' seems always to hold in reserve lines of thought or strands of argument that, as the reader presses on, pile up in a textual fabric that is experienced as beyond final fathoming. Philosophers priding themselves on the clarity of their thinking despised the obscure difficulty of his work. It seemed to be sheer obscurantism. Add to that the quasi-iconoclastic language, the language of deconstruction; this too seemed to many only to threaten to demolish or corrupt everything worth anything in an intellectual culture that had been cherished by scholars and students in the arts and humanities for hundreds of years. Derrida's view of language seemed to allow that as far as the interpretation of texts is concerned 'anything goes'. Moreover, it seemed to provide a theoretical reference point for anyone who wanted to pay exclusive attention to *non*-canonical texts and literatures, to everything that had hitherto been excluded by the 'hegemonic' authority of texts by Dead White European Men. (You know: Plato, Aristotle, St Augustine, Montaigne, Descartes, Leibniz, Rousseau, Kant, Hegel, Nietzsche, Marx, Husserl, Heidegger, Levinas, and so on. . . .)

On top of all this, or through all of this, Derrida's text touches a nerve. Some things one thinks about are states of affairs in the world, states of affairs with respect to which one can feel very varied and sometimes very violent emotions: happy, sad, angry, frightened, and so on. However, some matters for thinking are closer to home. To put it in the terms of the philosopher Martin Heidegger, they concern not the way the world one is in happens to be, but the way in which one understands one's own being-in-the-world. The angry resistance of conservative sensibilities to (let's call it) a 'political' effort to make changes to the world is nothing compared to the aggressive resistance that can be mustered to (let's call it) an 'ethical' effort to call into question our understanding of the world and the significance of our lives. This distinction between the ethical and the merely political is not really satisfactory. Derrida's text, in any case, does not everywhere respect it. Nevertheless, what I am saying is that his text invited not merely angry reactions but red-hot aggressive ones. And sometimes the heat all but obscured the light.

For example, they said at the time that it was 'the Derrida affair'. But it was a Cambridge affair, and beyond.

At the meeting of the Cambridge University Congregation in March 1992, an objection to one of the nominations for an honorary degree, the degree of *doctor honoris causa*, was lodged by the audible cry of '*non placet*' ('not content'). A ballot of the Regent House was organized, fly-sheets were circulated and signed. And on a Saturday in the middle of May, over 500 members attended the Senate House to register their opinion, voting by personal signature. The ballot was secret, but as members waited for the result, it mattered where you stood and with whom you stood. Younger fellows were aware that older eyes were watching. It was a Cambridge affair. Yet, as the Regent House was deciding whether to award an honorary degree to Jacques Derrida, it was never simply so, or solely so.

Derrida's nomination for the degree of *doctor honoris causa* – a nomination that, with considerable symbolic significance, did not come from *inside* the Philosophy Faculty – had aroused strong feelings within the University, and the ensuing rumpus attracted wide interest from both the national and international media. Academic opposition to politicians receiving such degrees was rare but at least familiar enough – but to a philosopher? What was all the fuss about? News journalists have a professional duty to address a non-specialist audience, and may have found the dispute hard to pin down or simplify. They may have sought simplicity where there was none. But if they were in a hurry to sort it out and get to the bottom of the thing, they were not alone, and not alone finding themselves wading in thought-treacle. Indeed, one of the central reasons for the 'not content' complaints against Derrida was that it was widely felt that his work massively violated the standards of rigour and clarity that academia should uphold, represent, and publicly honour.

Whatever Derrida's 'deconstructionism' (as opponents liked to call the thing) was, it was capable of being made to represent all that was rotten in our intellectual culture. That is, no doubt, in part its fault. It relates to a fault in Derrida's text. However, as we shall see, it also relates to a fault – a fissure – in the intellectual culture, a fissure into which this fault seemed seamlessly to fall.

The idea of giving an honorary degree to Derrida was, for many, a step too far; honouring the very thing that academics should stand four-square against. Now, when I say that many academics – and indeed many commentators (academic or not) on the intellectual life of our culture – felt strongly that Derrida was not the sort of person who ought to receive an academic honour, I do not want to make this sound like they thought his work was wrong or confused or mistaken on fundamental points or objectionable for some other run-of-the-mill academic reason. No, they did not merely have objections to Derrida's work – they were *infuriated* by it, and protectively *incensed* by its dubious appeal to bright young minds. As the self-authorized champions of the classical heritage, the comparison will only grate those involved, but the aggressive denunciations and hostility directed at Derrida's work surely offers a contemporary glimpse into the frame of mind that led to Socrates being tried and convicted by the courts of democratic Athens on a charge of corrupting the youth and disbelieving in the ancestral gods.

I am among those whose youth – and beyond – was 'corrupted' by Derrida. So for me, what I see in the Cambridge affair (and the numerous cases like it that plagued Derrida's career) was not a display of academic integrity and intellectual honesty but academics ('*certain academics*' as Derrida typically carefully, fairly, but nevertheless pointedly stressed later) who dramatically violated the very standards of academic responsibility they sought to uphold and represent, and in whose name the '*non placet*' had been made in the first place.

While the intensity of aggressive opposition to Derrida was, in our time, unrivalled, the terms of criticism ranged against him were by no means new. Indeed, for the *non placeters* 'the Derrida affair' was playing out, in an admittedly extreme case, a familiar drama of British letters in its relation to 'Continental' contacts. As one Cambridge academic, Nicholas Denyer, put it, for Derrida's opponents the case with Derrida was ultimately to be understood as yet another example where a French thinker was being 'acclaimed by many British intellectuals in spite of reservations among their philosophically educated compatriots'. While Denyer's image of a 'fissure' within the British intellectual culture is apt, it is, I think, secondary to and largely explained by the fact that the same image informs the picture of the contemporary *philosophical* culture in general, a fissure which Denyer's observation implicitly affirms. For one might turn the tables to emphasize that those 'British' (or more precisely 'analytic') philosophers who opposed Derrida were not the first roundly to condemn the work of their 'Continental' colleagues, and in remarkably similar terms.

The template for the Cambridge criticism was thus well prepared for in the assumption of a wide gulf between 'analytic' and 'Continental' philosophy. So, however personal and personally offensive they may have seemed, the fly-sheet's condemnations – that, for example, Derrida's work could 'deprive the mind of its defences' and 'undermine the fundamental grounds which provide . . . for intellectual inquiry' – were, despite Derrida's singular notoriety, not really unique to the case. In what is actually far too common a trait to be dismissed as an occasional shortcoming on the part of the 'analytic' critics of what is called 'Continental' philosophy, a litany of charges were brought against Derrida *without citing a single supporting quote or reference* to his work. Now, *if* they were justified, these charges would seriously question the University's wisdom in conferring a degree on Derrida of any sort. *If* it was right to call his work 'stupid and ridiculous' or 'degenerate' in virtue of 'its contempt for argumentative rigour' and its 'barbarous neologisms and idiotic word-play', then, of course, it would be understandable if one despaired of one's supposedly intelligent colleagues and their 'appetite for known falsehood', and the '*non placet*' should have been cheered to the rafters of the Senate House.

But there was good reason why the *non placeters* did not quote from Derrida's work. There was good reason why the standards of scholarship and rigour they were claiming to defend were not, in this case, brought to bear. For, for all its risks and difficulties (and these are so considerable it is more than a little daunting even to think about writing a short – or long – introduction to his work), his opponents' *anxious scruples* are, I believe, *misunderstandings*.

And the fault lines in Derrida's text that lend his opponents' claims a ring of plausibility open up where the attempt is made by Derrida to make enigmatic certain habitual patterns of thinking, thought-programmes, that he regards as internal to philosophy, at least as it has typically been elaborated hitherto. It gives the impression that he denies something, something known to be true.

The Cambridge affair, which cannot be cleanly isolated from a dossier of other affairs before and since, soon spread beyond Cambridge, and beyond merely 'British' philosophical assessments. A letter was sent to *The Times*, signed by 19 analytic philosophers outside the UK, including the leading American analytic philosopher W. V. O. Quine. It repeated many of the charges of the *non placeters*. It also repeated the basic dereliction of scholarly duty: not a sentence was cited, no references were made, no analyses of argument or lines of criticism from Derrida's 'voluminous writings' were pursued. Two words in the letter *were* placed between quotation marks, implicitly suggesting Derrida as their source: it was claimed that Derrida's writings 'seem to consist in no small part of elaborate jokes and puns ("logical phallusies" and the like)', but as Derrida himself emphasized, this is a phrase which he has '*never* written'. Is it not a very serious deception to pass off as the work of a charlatan what is, in fact, specious invention?

As I have indicated, Derrida is not the first 'Continental' philosopher to have found himself on the receiving end of this kind of attack. Nevertheless, not only was the Cambridge affair over a degree of *doctor honoris causa* a particularly clear case of British (or more generally Anglophone) hostility to what it came to call 'Continental philosophy', but also a sadly typical example of the sort of violent attack that Derrida was to receive throughout his career. Indeed, while Derrida would regularly get caught up in wars of one kind or another against 'Continental philosophy' or 'postmodernism' or 'French theory' or 'poststructuralism', and many other more or less vague and unhelpful appellations giving rise to references to 'Derrida and his ilk' or 'Derrida et al.', placing him amongst a company of like-minded troublemakers who were out to destroy Western civilization, and while he was often dragged in as a good representative of everything bad – he was also regularly singled out. He was the worst. (In 1999, he was voted the most overrated philosopher of all time.) There was, and still is in some quarters, a special kind of Derrida-text-effect, an allergic reaction against his name and work that brings out the most aggressive and ill-humoured reactions from academics, from journalists, from Britain, from America, from France too, and Germany – everywhere. Derrida, *bête noire*, peddler of fraudulent obscurantist rubbish, a danger to young impressionable minds. Young people keen to follow the most 'radical' thinkers, keen to stand apart from the herd, were wasting their youthful energies on Derrida's relativist, obscurantist, onanist texts.

For myself, I would be proud to be considered his ilk. And for Derrida's supporters in Cambridge in 1992, there was a happy ending to the affair. The Regent House vote went with the nomination, and later that year he was duly awarded the degree.

One of the most evident faults in Derrida's text is around the name 'philosophy' itself. Like the German thinker Martin Heidegger, whose texts were perhaps his most continuous reference, Derrida did not suppose his work to be bringing traditional philosophy to an end. Rather, something like an interminable task of thinking 'after philosophy' is brought into view in his work; a task that would open the philosophical heritage (which will have typically presented itself as heading towards an *end*) to its own 'beyond'. If we were to give the title 'philosophy' to Derrida's texts, this, on the one hand, seems appropriate, since most of his work is dedicated to inhabiting, in a new way, the philosophical heritage. On the other hand, conferring this title is also an inappropriate gesture. As we shall see, the ambition in Derrida's text is to give philosophy a future, but this is not the future that philosophy will have typically given itself (viz. the triumphant achievement of complete conceptual clarity), and so is perhaps best understood, as Ludwig Wittgenstein once proposed for his work, 'as one of the heirs of the subject which used to be called philosophy'.

On one occasion, Derrida introduced himself in the following, I believe extremely helpful, terms: 'I am by profession a philosopher, a teacher of philosophy. But I am not a philosopher through and through.' As a matter of fact, Derrida did not think that anyone could be a philosopher 'through and through', a philosopher who is in every part a philosopher. So when he says he is not a philosopher through and through, this does not single him out; it makes him like the rest. However, Derrida's 'but' indicates that he wants to mark a departure from what one might think when one thinks about those who are, by profession, philosophers. What philosophers might think is that they really are philosophers through and through. Their work is, in every sense, and throughout, *properly disciplined*. And on this point, there will be some measure of agreement with Derrida by philosophers who think they know what philosophy is and how to do it in a properly and thoroughly disciplined way. He is not sufficiently philosophical. In particular, his work is at odds with a properly philosophical conception of what it is for philosophical writing to be well shaped and disciplined. Indeed, he may even be an exemplary case of such indiscipline, a model for no one to follow. (Despite, or even in view of, the indignity of such an insult, I am not sure that Derrida would have to refuse this title. Like Kierkegaard and Wittgenstein, thinkers who knew that there would be effects of repetition as a result of their work, Derrida did not seek to spare other people the trouble of thinking.)

The objection to Derrida's work on the grounds of its indiscipline is not just an objection to its style. On the contrary, since one's *way of writing philosophy* cannot be independent of what one understands *doing philosophy properly* to be, it expresses a concern that Derrida does not (even) begin properly, does not pursue the writing of philosophy sufficiently philosophically. It's not that it goes wrong. Indeed, the reason why it is appropriate to speak of objections as scruples is that deconstruction is regarded as ethically questionable, and so dubious to pursue; it's the wrong kind of thing altogether, wrong, as it were, through and through. So Derrida's philosophical critics think they know what (well-shaped and disciplined) philosophical writing should look like, and respond aggressively to writing which, quite precisely, regards the place and manner of its own commencement as a genuine question. Perhaps one can affirm this only when one comes to take very seriously that no text can be philosophical through and through, and that the aspiration to achieve a kind of philosophical purity or complete conceptual clarity is questionable – and questionable from within a text which wants to be a legitimate heir to the subject that used to be called 'philosophy', even if an heir for which concepts such as 'legitimate heir' are no longer something that can be taken for granted – indeed, even if for an inheritance for which the very structure of inheritance cannot be taken for granted.

It is a question of having to write philosophy in the condition in which writing philosophy has itself become a philosophical problem.

In the interview on photography that I introduced in the opening chapter, Derrida contrasts the foregrounding, or 'fetishization', of the author figure with what he wanted to understand as central to writing: 'writing', he says, 'means to withdraw oneself'. This gesture is, in fact, deeply traditional in philosophy, and is certainly central to the kind of inheritance of Descartes' philosophy that characterized the two thinkers with whom Derrida first engaged as a young academic, Edmund Husserl and Martin Heidegger. Husserl, for example, describes the condition of 'all modern philosophy' like this:

> All modern philosophy originates in the Cartesian *Meditations* . . . This historical proposition means that every genuine beginning of philosophy issues from meditations, from solitary self-reflection.

> Autonomous philosophy . . . comes into being in the solitary, radical taking responsibility for himself on the part of the philosopher. Through isolation and meditation alone does a philosopher come into being, does philosophy begin in him.

One might object that Husserl's formulation gives an overly individualistic construal of the condition of writing it aims to describe: the condition is one which seems to call for heroically creative acts *ex nihilo*. Nevertheless, there is, I think, an important and quite general truth in the picture of radical isolation presented in Husserl's description. It is that, even for those who today find certain ways of going on (Derrida's for example) departing from all philosophical propriety, even for those who find that the resources of philosophical writing typically available to them 'present themselves so strongly', as the British philosopher Bernard Williams puts it, 'as the responsible way of going on', the condition of inheritance in philosophy involves, for everyone and for each equally, an irrecusable responsibility. My being-an-heir to the subject that has been called 'philosophy' can never be reduced to the passive reception of something simply available (a given which presents itself strongly), and even those who endorse the currently dominant 'resources' do not do so, cannot do so, in utter ignorance of the fact that philosophy does not have one legitimate heir only. In question, then, is not the passive acquisition of a forceful fragment of what is typically available, but relatively confident acts of endorsement, what one might call the 'countersigning' of a particular way of going on. And the moment of such a countersignature is, I am suggesting, essentially a moment in which (even if one has numbers on one's side) one is on one's own.

Derrida wanted to be able to do what he could to withdraw best, to assume a certain solitude. The 'isolation' of the philosopher insisted upon here might seem to exclude anything like a communal character of philosophy. But that is not so. Rather, it specifies the nature of that community as, precisely, an *ethical* one, that is as a community of self-responsible singularities, a community without the common, a community, as Derrida came to put it, without community. Moreover, the idea of specifying writing in terms of a withdrawal from a certain publicness – the contemporary publicity set-up with its distinctive forms of visibility and associated media criteria of what counts as fit for public broadcast – is not in any case *any* kind of invitation to construe such solitude in terms of an 'egocentric predicament', in terms that is of an 'isolated' or 'worldless' subject, as has become the standard way of construing the lesson of a Cartesian meditation. A *leitmotif* of Derrida's conception of the character of lived existence as 'inscribed habitation' is a conception of our being as 'always already situated habitation'. We are, all of us, in a world already, already as Derrida would say 'in a text' which is immediately 'not private', not one's own alone. Being-in-the-world *is*, as Heidegger puts it, being-with-others. The Cartesian tradition of conceiving subjectivity, personality, and I-hood is constantly called into question in Derrida's work. On that conception, subjectivity is characterized by pure interiority, the purely non-mundane; an inner space of self-present consciousness. On such a view, the presence of others is always an epistemological problem. For Derrida, by contrast, 'the economy of one's own' being-in, the localization of one's own being-there, is a 'scriptural space' that is everywhere run through by an inherited culture and language one does not choose; the most intimate 'being at home with oneself' always already accommodates the trace of the other. And concrete relations to the other – ethics, politics, everyday hospitality – were always alive in Derrida's text too.

It should be clear already that in Derrida's text there is a marked effort to avoid a cult of any proper names, least of all his own, as if an author was a 'subject' present to his text and to what he wrote, the original creative genius at the origin of the texts he signs. Books written these days are often prefaced by long slews of grateful acknowledgements thanking everyone for everything but the errors. But, as we shall see, Derrida's acknowledgements tend to find their place *within* his texts and do not just precede them. For Derrida, acknowledgement of the other becomes of methodological and not merely personal significance. One might compare this to Gilbert Ryle's book *The Concept of Mind*. Although that text is deservedly known for the way it opposes a Cartesian construal of subjectivity, its textuality, in another way, affirms it. Famously it has no footnotes at all and no texts by others are appealed to or cited anywhere (not even Descartes'). Less often recalled is that the book has no acknowledgements either. Ryle states instead that he is 'primarily' trying to 'get some disorders out of my own system', and only 'secondarily' interested in helping others. One might also recall here, Ryle's response at a conference on the topic of 'analytic philosophy' in France in the late 1950s where, upon being asked whether his position was 'strictly in agreement' with 'the programme outlined at the beginning of the century by Russell and refined by Wittgenstein and some others', he vehemently replied: '*I certainly hope not*'. The methodological significance of this remark is important. Despite his resistance to the Cartesian 'myths' of isolated consciousness, on the one hand, and of an uninhabited world, on the other, Ryle's text is constructed with a strong sense of its author as solitary in just the way Derrida resists: as the sole resident, as it were, of an inner fortress.

While Derrida's text is not in form or content marked by a withdrawal to an individual 'subject' conceived as isolated in that condition, he associates the appearance of the writer with a certain mode of disappearance from conventional forms of visibility and publicness. The thought here is that when it comes to getting *oneself* across in one's *singularity*, when it comes to giving one's thoughts the best chance of bearing a stamp of one's own commitments, 'the writer absents himself better, that is expresses himself better as other, addresses himself to the other more effectively than the man of speech'. Jacques Derrida wanted to withdraw from a certain mode of publicness and of the model of the public intellectual, but for reasons we will see in due course, the withdrawal does not disclose the singularity of his being-there as an individual resident of a secure and impenetrable inner fortress, but, rather, as a singular point of confluence, a point of remarkable hospitality to the other, a generous gathering place. Exploiting the derivation of 'in' from archaic German '*innan*', meaning 'to reside', 'to dwell', 'habitation', and which is likely to be comparable to English 'inn', we might attempt to construe 'Derrida's text' in terms of an exemplary mode of being-inn. Not an atom but an hospitable node. And what a node . . .

After you

The points just made about acknowledgement are an illustration of a performative dimension that seems always to mark Derrida's texts; namely, the consistent attempt to respect what the text says in the very way it goes about saying it. However, as is perhaps already evident, this performative consistency can also make Derrida's texts head-spinningly multi-layered, unfathomable, unreadable – and un-introducible. And, as we are beginning to see, readers are divided over whether or not to regard the experienced difficulty of reading Derrida's writings as a positive virtue of their formatting.

One sympathetic reader has suggested that this kind of effect of Derrida's work renders its impact on one as akin to 'something that goes bump in the day'. This is what I meant when, in the opening chapter, I said that Derrida's text touches a nerve, and is why his work has been so prominently marked by responses ranging from the derogatory to the adulatory, why he was both, as he put it, 'excluded *and* favourite'. There is a resistance and an attraction on the part of us all to finding enigmatic what we more commonly find matter of course. In responding to Derrida, one of these reactions tends to come to the fore at the expense of the other. Those who take the line of greatest resistance find him digestible, if digestible at all, only by first re-processing his thought into something more tractable, usually something to the effect that Derrida was a kind of sceptical nihilist who doubts that texts mean anything or who affirms that all statements are of equal value or who thinks that as far as interpretation of meaning is concerned anything goes.

One such reader of Derrida, and a reader who clearly takes the time actually to study Derrida's text, is Gavin Kitching. Following a distinctively Wittgensteinian path of resistance to certain tempting steps in philosophy, Kitching attempts to show that the kind of high-wire textual performances that so delight Derrida's more impressionable readers are the upshot of ground-floor conceptual errancy. It is not a rigorously consistent text but the spiralling into orbit of language that has simply lost touch with itself, language that has lost its connection to our life with language. There is, as a result, Kitching argues, a peculiar emptiness or idleness to Derrida's text. And this is something that can be exposed when we realize that, in the face of the fog that descends when we try to follow its high-wire antics, 'we do not know what to say in response'.

I think that Kitching's effort at making vivid this sense of the 'fog' surrounding Derrida's work inadvertently help us to lift some of it. And since fog has served to isolate many readers from the Derridean continent, this is also a good place to begin a more detailed journey into his writings. The discussion of Kitching's concerns will ultimately conjoin Derrida with Wittgenstein in a way I find congenial, and I hope this might also give Kitching (indeed anyone, me for example) pause for further thinking.

The especially helpful thing about Kitching's discussion is that it presents Derrida in terms which are largely continuous with the public image that grew up around his work. According to Kitching, the central Derridean theoretical 'generalization' is that all 'meaning in language' is inherently *ambiguous* and hence that we can never establish with certainty what a text (for example, what someone says) means. It is this thesis that so undermines the standards of rigour cherished by Derrida's opponents. All efforts to understand a text, to explore and assess claims, to advance truths, all this requires that there is something to be understood, something asserted, something capable of assessment, criticism, appreciation, enjoyment, disagreement, and so on. If, on the other hand, there is no such thing as 'what a text means', if it can always be interpreted in a multitude of different ways, then the scholarly aspiration to understand a text or to achieve some kind of clarity about what it means explodes in a puff of postmodern objections to elites and canons and hegemonies. On such a view, any effects of meaning will either be constituted by subjective meaning-giving acts of a free reader, or (on a more darkly political conception) by the dominant powers that be. In any case, the idea of a pedagogical or scholarly reading of exemplary texts in different genres – the kind of reading practice, whether traditional or critical, that has been cultivated by the humanities – is totally undermined. If all 'meaning in language' is inherently ambiguous, then any understanding we can legitimately aspire to is merely a resigned sense that any attempt to establish legitimacy is just an act of violence of some kind.

To try to show how radically unclear the supposed Derridean 'generalization' is, Kitching brings things down to earth, away from complex theoretical or literary texts, and imagines or recalls text events or speech acts for which he is confident that things are clear: first, an occasion when someone really is unsure what another person means, and, second, in contrast to this, and what he insists is anyway 'more commonly' the case, namely, an occasion when someone is 'absolutely clear' what another person means. In the latter kind of case, Kitching claims, there is 'no ambiguity of meaning there at all' and the listener typically grasps the speaker's meaning 'immediately'.

Kitching supposes then that while some examples seem to speak for Derrida's generalization, others – many, many more others – would seem to speak against it. What remains totally unclear, and this is Kitching's point, is Derrida's generalization itself. It is a 'form of idling language' that, try as one might, one cannot but fail to get one's head round.

I think Kitching is right to suppose that Derrida affirms *something like* a general 'ambiguity of meaning'. We will have to stress the 'something like' qualification, however, since Derrida explicitly *contrasts* the word he uses to characterize the phenomenon at issue, what he calls 'dissemination', with the traditional concept of 'polysemia', the concept of multiple meanings. Nevertheless, the idea that the meaning of an expression is *always susceptible* to 'internal shifting' in different contexts does seem to capture something that, as Kitching puts it, 'Derrida insists' on.

So let us closely examine the example that Kitching gives with respect to which, he conclusively concludes, 'Derrida clearly wrong'. It is a wonderful example, one that Derrida would have wanted to examine at far greater length than I can here.

> I think, for example, of holding the door open for an elderly female colleague and saying 'After you'. She walked through the door ahead of me. She did not say, for example 'After me? I'd be surprised. Nobody's been after me for years.' She got my meaning immediately, but she might not have done. After all, the latter might have been an appropriate, even witty or flirtatious, reply to my words. But on the other hand, no. Such a reply would precisely have been witty because she knew, as I knew, that 'after you' said in that context is an invitation to precede the speaker through the door. No ambiguity of meaning there at all. The 'action context', as it were, clarified all in that case. Derrida clearly wrong.

The example is, I should think, of a fairly common type. The wonderful little text 'After you' is a very everyday machine, and it is clear that Kitching knows how to operate it. In particular, he knows – and his elderly female colleague knows too – that it can be used as 'an invitation to precede the speaker through the door'.

Moreover, in the 'action context' we are presented with, that is exactly how it is used. Kitching knows this little machine well enough to know how it might be wittily taken, in addition, as an abbreviation of 'I'm after you'. And no doubt he could have himself invented a context in which an even more similar-sounding – indeed to the ear indistinguishable – machine could have functioned differently again. For example, in a rather different contextual scenario between two elderly farming colleagues, one might hear a concluding agreement for each one to take 'arf der ewe'. But, as Kitching says, no. In the 'action context' he is imagining, the little machine functions as 'an invitation to precede the speaker through the door'. Other machines might have done that job for him too. He could have said, for example, 'You go first' or 'Do precede me through the door' or 'I invite you to precede me through the door'. In this case, he used the more elegant 'After you', and there was no misunderstanding: 'She got my meaning immediately'. 'Derrida clearly wrong' – right?

Well, no, I don't think so. What I think Kitching's example shows is that Kitching wants to regards *his own concept* of 'understanding a sentence' as *exhausted* by this idea of *knowing how it might be used*. Indeed, according to Kitching, saying 'After you' in this context, *is* nothing over and above 'an invitation to precede the speaker through the door'. That's why it can be so immediately understood. There's nothing else to *get* about it. And I do think Derrida's affirmation of 'dissemination' – which, as the word implies, is meant to suggest the dispersal of the 'seme' as a unit of meaning – challenges that construal. He will want to say there *always* is *something else to get*. And getting at that requires a sensitivity that is not reducible to the know-how of 'knowing how the sentence might be used'. Specifically, it requires a sensitivity to getting *what it is about* that is not given even if the use is given. But can this really be said in Kitching's everyday example? Surely, here there is nothing more to *get* than is given by 'knowing how the sentence might be used'?

To help see what Derrida wants to affirm in the affirmation of 'dissemination', I want to consider the following sentence:

> He held a door open for an elderly female colleague and said 'After you'.

Do I understand this sentence? Surely it would make a difference to my understanding if, in the narrative within which it was laid down, we were told that the elderly female colleague addressed by Kitching was an utterly charmless misanthrope. Or if it transpired that she had just publicly criticized Kitching in a meeting. Or if it transpired that she was really Kitching's fantasy of an elderly female colleague. Or if it transpired that she was Kitching's fantasy of himself as such a female colleague. I am not introducing any ambiguity here. In the sense in which Kitching understands it, there is none. But I think it is clear that each of these variations might lead us to *understand what this sentence is about* differently. Indeed, we can affirm that *and* accept that the expression 'After you' could, in each case, be replaced by another kind of invitation to precede him through the door. What is no longer so clear or obvious, however, is that the one who is addressed here 'immediately understands' the sentence on that account. On the contrary, here as everywhere, even when the use is given, it still makes sense to speak of finding something not yet 'readable' in the sentence, and hence of it remaining still to be read. To sharpen that point, let's imagine a brief continuation of Kitching's scene:

> He held a door open for an elderly female colleague and said 'After you'. After he had said this, he left her as he did the day before.

Are you now so convinced that when he said 'After you', 'she got [his] meaning immediately'? And what about the following continuation?

> He held a door open for an elderly female colleague and said 'After you'. After he had said this, he followed her as he did the day before.

Again, can we affirm that when he said 'After you' to her it is 'absolutely clear' that 'she got [his] meaning immediately'? These are just two paths, and really there are *countless* contexts into which one might graft this little text machine. And in each case, without exploiting any (countable) semantic ambiguity in the sense of the expression (this has nothing to do with ambiguity in the sense of polysemia), we might want to say we understand it *differently*. This is what Derrida means by 'dissemination' and it is not, in Derrida's account, just a (happy or unhappy) fact of linguistic life that we have to put up with and which someone might now and then exploit with an independently specifiable linguistic instrument. On the contrary, as we shall see, this possibility of grafting a textual form into (strictly countless) different contextual chains is, according to Derrida, fundamental to its *being* the textual form it is. In this account, the emphasis is on the openness of the grafted material to expressing something new, something sufficiently singular that it more commonly resists 'immediate understanding'. By contrast, Kitching's approach to someone operating with the words 'After you' is one which would rather construe the scene as 'more commonly' one in which 'I am absolutely clear that you mean this and not that in language and that they meant this and not that in language'. It is a construal which wants to leave nothing in this text to be desired, nothing singular in it *yet to come*.

And in doing so, he passes over that which, in *his own concept* of understanding, he might have sometimes preferred to affirm. One might also note that this is something that Wittgenstein, whose ideas on the use of sentences in his book *Philosophical Investigations* form the background to Kitching's argument, tried to teach us to avoid. As you will see from the following sequence of remarks from that book, I have been pulling Kitching's example towards another Wittgensteinian path already. Indeed, one of the sentences I used in extending Kitching's scene came from Wittgenstein himself, and his theme is precisely whether what we call 'understanding a sentence' is exclusively a matter of knowing how it might be used:

> 'After he had said this, he left her as he did the day before.' – Do I understand this sentence? Do I understand it just as I should if I heard it in the course of a narrative? If it were set down in isolation I should say, I don't know what it's about. But all the same I should know how this sentence might be used; I could myself invent a context for it.
>
> (A multitude of familiar paths lead off from these words in every direction.)
>
> We speak of understanding a sentence in the sense in which it can be replaced by another which says the same; but also in the sense in which it cannot be replaced by any other. (Any more than one musical theme can be replaced by another.)
>
> Then has 'understanding' two different meanings here? – I would rather say that these kinds of use of 'understanding' make up its meaning, make up my *concept* of understanding. For I *want* to apply the word 'understanding' to all this.
>
> *Hearing* a word in a particular sense. How queer that there should be such a thing!
>
> Phrased *like this*, emphasized like this, heard in this way, this sentence is the first of a series in which a transition is made to *these* sentences, pictures, actions.
>
> ((A multitude of familiar paths lead off from these words in every direction.))

I have contracted the sequence of remarks somewhat, in part for the sake of brevity. However, I hope there is enough here to engage in a work of reading Kitching's wanting to apply the word 'understanding' to only part of his concept.

I have also contracted the sequence of Wittgenstein's remarks enough to see at a glance the recurrence of *the dissemination-affirming phrase* 'A multitude of familiar paths lead off from these words in every direction'. What is achieved by the repetition of the very same sentence? Does Wittgenstein find it *irreplaceably* fitting? Does it function in the same way in both remarks or make the same point? Why the doubling of parentheses in the second case? Is this just a question of style? I do not raise these questions because I know already how to answer them confidently or authoritatively, but because I don't. And I am drawing attention to Kitching's reductive conception of what is 'more commonly' the case precisely because one would think that his own very long-run effort at coming to terms with Wittgenstein might have itself invited a consideration of this time with a text. Why does he overlook the fact that what he calls his 'Wittgensteinian education' involved reading and reading and reading and reading again the writings of the later Wittgenstein? Kitching describes the 'journey' as 'quasi-autobiographical', a point which he pointedly connects to the fact that the movements of orientation and re-orientation which have marked his journey matter to him sufficiently deeply that he can 'wince' and be 'embarrassed' by the forms of 'thinking and feeling' he formerly accepted. At issue here is precisely not a matter of 'getting the meaning immediately' but a movement in which Kitching developed, changed, and worked over an *understanding* of Wittgenstein's text that was, in his view, frequently 'at least to some degree . . . a *misunderstanding*'. Has the journey of this quasi-autobiographical movement nothing to do with the way the *Philosophical Investigations* is written? And if the objection is that such a text is radically atypical and far from common and that 'more commonly' one is 'absolutely clear' that others 'meant this and not that' by their words, then it would seem to be Kitching himself who is more attracted to what one might call 'metaphysical' construals (let's say of wanting to speak 'absolutely') of what 'more commonly' goes on '*in* language, *in* life, *in* context'.

It is that 'metaphysical' construal of the everydayness of one's life with language that Derrida wants to call into question. Indeed, he clearly invites us to wonder at what we want when we want to define as 'more commonly' the case a reception of the words of an other construed in terms of the concept of an *immediately* grasped meaning. As we shall see in the next chapter, Derrida identifies his 'final intention' in the work undertaken in *Of Grammatology* (but certainly not only there) to be 'to make enigmatic' what one thinks one understands by words like 'immediacy' or 'proximity' or 'presence'. Perhaps especially what we like to think we understand by them immediately.

Chapter 3
Reading the logocentric heritage

At the end of the last chapter, I introduced what Derrida calls the 'final intention' of his groundbreaking work *Of Grammatology*. It is not a matter of wanting to *deny* (or indeed of wanting to *affirm*) the correctness of our naive, normal way of expressing ourselves, but of helping us to find remarkable what he thinks we tend, in philosophy, to find insufficiently so. What he develops in that book is a 'theoretical matrix' that, he hopes, can assist in this task; to open the space for a new way of reading the philosophical heritage, its dominant structures and patterns of thinking, revealing its systematic dependence on (what will now appear to be an insufficiently critical appeal to) concepts like 'immediacy', 'proximity', and 'presence'. Inhabiting the philosophical heritage '*in a certain way*', making inventive and selective use of certain parts of the old structure, Derrida seeks to articulate the movements within it which take it on to another heading; to give it a future.

This point is worth underlining. Derrida, understood by many as a sceptical nihilist, was received with horror by some. Others, however, delighted in the possibility of finding in what was becoming known as 'deconstruction' something like the radical destruction of the European philosophical heritage. In response to this reception, Derrida's text began to insist more expressly that the work of reading being elaborated in the name of deconstruction did not involve a rejection of the heritage:

> I love very much everything that I deconstruct in my own manner; the texts I want to read from the deconstructive point of view are texts I love, with that impulse of identification which is indispensable for reading. They are texts whose future, I think, will not be exhausted for a long time . . . Plato's signature is not yet finished . . . – nor is Nietzsche's, nor is St Augustine's.

Slowly readers began to learn that Derrida did not write in a 'critical fury' against the philosophical heritage, but for the sake of that heritage, out of love for it, concerned above all to forge a future for it – a future for it beyond its own anticipated future.

And yet, as we have seen, the standard misunderstandings of Derrida's text correspond to fault lines within it. His work pushes our current capacity for (self-)understanding to the limits of tolerance, openly resisting every effort to wrap it up in philosophically familiar dress-codes, and thereby resisting 'immediate understanding'. The upshot, to take a term from Roland Barthes, is a text of a profoundly and sometimes frustratingly *writerly* type. This term characterizes kinds of texts which do not conform to a reader's ordinary expectations concerning what well-disciplined writing of a certain type or genre (whether this is a novel or a philosophical text) should look like. The resources already available to us for reading Derrida's text really seem to give us a kind of structural incompetence in coming to terms with what is going on in them, with what they are about.

On the one hand, then, we may unwittingly fall back on inappropriate interpretive keys (scepticism, relativism, nihilism) for reading a philosophical text that is doing something new. So we need to be warned against concluding too quickly that we know what is emerging in the work of reading the philosophical heritage pursued in the name of 'deconstruction'. Our inherited ways of coming to terms with a philosophical text can stand in the way of letting us become better – less standardly awful – readers of Derrida's. Indeed, coming to terms with this extra-ordinary philosophical resource cannot but involve readers learning to find their inherited philosophical resources as an obstacle as well as an interpretive aid in reading them. On the other hand, however, the reader's interpretive task is not utterly hopeless, even if it is never utterly over. A contribution to our heritage which is not content to leave nothing within it to be desired, nothing still to be thought, nothing singular in it *yet to come*, a contribution to the heritage worthy of the name, will itself offer guidance to becoming a reader of that contribution.

So while I am ruefully sure that our finding it hard to make headway in the remarkable textual environments that Derrida has left us is internal to their formation – it is a stubbornly unrevisable feature/fissure in its formation – I am also sure that learning how to endure ongoing struggles of not knowing your way about, of not knowing 'what it really means', and of re-learning what 'wanting to know what it means' might mean, is part of a Derridean education too. In the first part of this chapter, I aim to explore a text in which the pitfalls and the ambitions that lie ahead of the reader might be expected to be most carefully and helpfully anticipated: the preface to Derrida's breakthrough text *Of Grammatology*. In the second part, I will follow the first tentative steps that follow that preface: Derrida's astonishing effort to make visible nothing short of *a new mutation in the history of the world*.

A preface to what remains to come

Of Grammatology begins with a preface, just over a page long. It is quite a traditional preface in that it states without more ado what the author intends to do. Yet that conformity to the norm also makes it engage with a more or less traditional philosophical problem with prefaces, at least since Hegel asked his readers not to take him seriously in his. The supposed problem with prefaces is that the '*prae-fatio*' is a saying-before-hand that is actually written-after-the-fact, after the work, and as standing outside the (real) work of the work, that real work thus being the essential '*prae-fatio*' of writing the preface. Derrida does not dwell on this logic of the preface in the preface to *Of Grammatology*. However, in an over 50-page-long preface to a book published five years later, *Dissemination*, the status of the preface does become an explicit theme, and Derrida's later remarks helpfully preface the earlier apparently more traditional ones:

> The preface announces in the future tense ('this is what you are going to read') the conceptual content or significance of what will already have been written. And thus sufficiently read to be gathered up in its semantic tenor and proposed in advance. From [this] viewpoint, which re-creates an intention-to-say after the fact, the [main] text exists as something written – a past – which, under the false appearance of a present, a hidden omnipotent author (in full mastery of his product) is presenting to the reader as his future. 'Here it is what I wrote, then read, and what I am writing that you are going to read. After which you will again be able to take possession of the preface which in sum you have not yet begun to read, even though, once having read it, you will have already anticipated everything that follows and thus you might just as well dispense with reading the rest.'

The 'pre' of the pre-face makes the future present, a future which is in fact already written and past. One might wonder then whether there can really be a preface to what remains to come that does not render what remains to come everything except, precisely, 'to come'. Perhaps only if what remains to come will have always already resisted an idea of '*complete* gathering up' that a writer of a preface or indeed a writer of a system of philosophy might yearn for.

Of Grammatology begins, as I say, with a short preface. In it, Derrida tells us, very straightforwardly, what we will read and announces 'the guiding intention' of the book. This he then describes in terms of the problematization (or making problematic) of traditional approaches to the 'critical reading' of texts (consequent it later transpires upon considerations surrounding the status of *writing* throughout the history, especially, of philosophy, but we will come back to that), a problematization which will require, he states, a radical adjustment in 'classical' conceptions of the shape of human history. Indeed, it will 'demand that reading should free itself . . . from the classical categories of history'. Although Derrida does not take this to involve the abandonment or rejection of 'classical norms' concerning, for example, periodization in historical research, it will attempt to make problematic or enigmatic the idea of history as unfolding (perhaps in distinct periods, stages, or ages or epochs) as a linear development towards a definite end; an idea that still underlies efforts to chart the historical course that leads to our 'modern' time.

Unlike most today who want to understand what is going on in our 'today', Derrida takes seriously the extent to which our historical understanding is indebted to a distinctively philosophical tradition: a philosophical tradition which conceives human history as a whole as a goal-directed, or 'teleological', movement in stages from a primitive, or 'savage', animal origin towards an ideal, fully human, end of man and end of history to come. Derrida will typically regard this tradition as including all the great metaphysical systems of the Western canon and will claim, somewhat surprisingly I would think, that this conception of history has always been configured by a distinctive interpretation of the history of *writing*. And so Derrida's reflections on what writing is – his new 'grammatological project' – will, in effect, aim to intervene at the very heart of the classical philosophical tradition as he reads it, a tradition that, in his view, still profoundly marks the self-understanding of our 'today'. Derrida's resistance to the linear and teleological norm of classic philosophical history of the world belongs centrally to his effort to open up another heading for philosophy, a not so teleological heading, as we shall see. Going back behind the oppositions through which we have typically understood ourselves for centuries hitherto, Derrida's new 'science of writing' will no longer be dominated by even that most traditionally radical of all period-breakers: 'the opposition of nature and culture, animality and humanity, etc.'. The entire conceptuality through which we have come to understand the entity that we ourselves are – the idea of capital 'M' 'Man' and the idea of a proper 'end of Man' – will be called into question.

The scope of this analysis is unbelievably wide. And yet, it is tempered with a modesty that deserves stressing. Wanting to 'respect classical norms' while at the same time endeavouring inventively to strike a path which will challenge the founding resources of modern Western thought is not something Derrida claims to be able to pursue 'without embarrassing [himself] in the process'. And as I hope to show in the rest of this section, Derrida's work of re-reading the heritage of Western modernity cannot avoid this embarrassment. This is not simply because his work inevitably produces hard-to-bear conceptual fissures and faults in our self-understanding (which it does) but rather because such fissures and faults inevitably multiply and accumulate in a text that can *itself* only be written as a kind of preface to what remains to come. As we shall see, Derrida's engagement with Western modernity has as its guiding light an openness to a 'future world' that cannot be reduced to anything presently live or immediately available in our time (irreducible, for example, to a present anticipation or expectation of a future present). How such a future that remains 'to come' can serve as a *guide* to research pursued 'here and now' is not something that such research will be able unproblematically to articulate in the terms of philosophy's traditional guidance on the relationship between, for example, guidance and light. What guides Derrida is not the light of a vision of a truly human future – a future in which we have *finally* learned how to live – but the impetus or impulse (in the 'here and now') of a commitment, a promise, or a pledge to contrive a 'heading' which does not set its sights on such a final end of Man. As he puts it, 'if there is a categorical imperative, it consists in doing everything for the future to remain open'. I will continue to work towards a clarification of this idea in what follows.

Of Grammatology is divided into two parts. Part I is entitled 'Writing Before the Letter' and 'outlines', as I have said, 'a theoretical matrix'. This grid of connected ideas is intended to serve to justify the effort at a 'rehabilitation of writing' that will provide a lever for a new interpretation or reading of the history of philosophy. Part II is entitled 'Nature, Culture, Writing' and engages with the task of going back behind traditional Western thinking about the history of the world through an analysis of its singular expression in the work of Rousseau.

Part I begins with a short text of just over two pages enigmatically (for me at least) entitled 'Exergue', a text which is led off by the following series of three numbered quotations, forming, Derrida says, 'a triple exergue':

1. The one who will shine in the science of writing will shine like the sun. A scribe (EP, p. 87)

   O Samas (sun-god), by your light you can scan the totality of lands as if they were cuneiform signs (ibid.)

2. These three ways of writing correspond almost exactly to three different stages according to which one can consider men gathered into a nation. The depicting of objects is appropriate to a savage people; signs of words and of propositions, to a barbaric people; and the alphabet to civilised people. J.-J. Rousseau, *Essai sur l'origine des langues*

3. Alphabetic script is in itself and for itself the most intelligent. Hegel, *Enzyklopadie*

The first numbered 'exergue' is formed from two sayings which originate from sources before even classical antiquity. They are sayings of the ancients that Derrida sourced from

L'écriture et la psychologie des peuples (referred to here by Derrida as 'EP') one of the two books that were the focus for a long review essay written in 1965 from which *Of Grammatology* was, in its first part, worked up. Together, these ancient sayings anticipate the project of Derrida's own grammatology (his own 'science of writing') and, since we have just noted a moment of modesty, indicate the frankly astonishing extent of his ambition. The second numbered 'exergue' of the triplet represents a profoundly *ethnocentric* (by which Derrida intends to pick out analyses which affirm a certain superiority of what is called 'Western Man' over every other human group) and *phonocentric* (by which Derrida intends to pick out analyses which affirm a certain priority to what is called 'speech' over what is called 'writing') conception of the history of writing, anticipating what Derrida will present as Rousseau's exemplary position in the 'age' or 'epoch' that he (Derrida) wants to delimit as ours and which we still inhabit. And if we anticipate that the kind of *intelligence* supposedly unique to 'Man' has been determined over and over again in the history of philosophy as the capacity for grasping a *pure order of intelligibility*, or ideal '*logos*', then the third numbered 'exergue', from Hegel, anticipates that the *ethnocentric* and *phonocentric* conception is also *logocentric* (by which Derrida intends to pick out analyses which affirm a certain irreducibility of what are called 'ideal meanings').

Following the triplet of quotations, Derrida tells us what his point is in quoting them, or what they are 'intended . . . to focus attention on'. We need to read the next page very carefully because Derrida spells it out *very* slowly. What the 'triple exergue' announces or is intended to focus attention on is:

(a) '*not only*' a marked *ethnocentricism* connected with the concept of *phonetic* writing

and

(b) '*nor merely*' a marked *logocentrism* which, he claims, constantly controls (and yet is *also* – in a certain way – constantly challenged by)

   i) *the concept of writing* in a world where the phoneticization of writing must dissimulate its own history

   ii) *the history of metaphysics* which has always assigned the origin of truth in general to the *logos*, and

   iii) *the concept of science*

   and

(c) '*not only*' announce that a science of writing, grammatology, is showing signs of liberation all over the world

but, with this 'triple exergue', finally,

(d) '*above all*' to suggest that a science of writing runs the risk of never being established as such (there could be for it, for example, no unity of a project, no statement of method, no statement of limits and so on). And that is because the very idea of such a science as one which would liberate us from an age dominated by logocentric patterns of thinking, the very idea of this science 'is meaningful for us' only *within* that age and that domination.

As I have indicated, however, the fact that Derrida had his days in that age too did not stop him attempting to make more or less systematic steps or simply stop him in his theoretical tracks with regard to a new grammatological project. So he concludes with a final (and characteristically cautious)

(e) '*Perhaps*', 'perhaps a patient meditation and painstaking investigation on and around what is still provisionally called writing' may still be a way of being 'faithful to a future world', a future that we cannot anticipate in the present, a future

> beyond every present horizon of anticipation or foresight, but which nevertheless has a kind of *imminence* that 'proclaims itself at present'.

No doubt this future world would be one in which the classic (Western) understanding of the history of the world and the significance of human life no longer dominates (and hence, if Derrida is right, 'the values of sign, word, and writing' will have been 'put into question' too). However, in so far as the 'future world' is precisely *not* a future that we can anticipate within the horizon of the present world, a future world 'beyond the closure of knowledge', one will have to admit that 'for that future world . . . for that which guides our future anterior, there is as yet no exergue'.

The logic of the preface was at work all along. However, with *Of Grammatology* we have a case of a preface-like work that will not have already been pre-faced by the work it prefaces. Perhaps, nevertheless, we can *hope* that this preface-like work *will have been* faithful to that future world. This is Derrida's 'messianic' hope, a messianism *without* a determinate messianism: for this is a hope that hopes precisely for a future world that is no longer dominated by the classic hope for a coming final end. This is the slightly head-spinning idea mentioned earlier of a 'heading' that cannot (and must not) be construed as a heading towards the final 'end of Man'; a telos for 'us' that would not be just one more anthropic telos. Deconstruction, for Derrida, makes its way through an inventive movement towards a future in which the very idea of the movement into the future is conceived in a radically new – and not so teleological – way. Not just a new heading or another heading for Man, but a heading that would be something other than a heading for Man, a heading in which the future remains, precisely, open, to come. The significance (and I mean that in the literal as well as in the evaluative sense of that word) of Derrida's work is thus far from assured since its production is *premised* on a commitment to the future to come 'beyond the closure of knowledge'. Nevertheless, Derrida wagers –

places a bet on himself – that his writings on writing, 'are the wanderings of a way of thinking' that will have been a preface to what remains to come.

In later writings, Derrida calls the 'political' idea encoded in such a messianic hope, the hope 'beyond' Western ethnocentrism *and* anti-ethnocentrism, 'democracy to come'. However, even this (apparently familiar) designation does not really pretend to be able to specify a positive 'destination' of a future to come. As Derrida puts it, what speaks for calling it 'democracy' is a fold within hope itself: the fact that it embodies a commitment, or 'pledge', to 'open out to the future':

> For democracy remains to come; this is its essence *in so far as it remains*: not only will it remain indefinitely perfectible, hence always insufficient and future, but belonging to the time of the promise, it will always remain, in each of its future times to come.

So Derrida is not invoking the idea of the future world as something which guides him as an idea or ideal of a looked-forward-to future present. Nevertheless, he does want his own work to be the expression of a promise or commitment; it belongs to an attempt to act 'here and now' that, as it were, sends itself forward in a way that is future-producing. Hence the 'in so far as it remains' of 'democracy to come' involves an essential reference to something – let's call it deconstruction – that already takes place *now*. What are we to make of this? Without doubt, the temporal torsion implied by this 'now' of 'democracy to come' makes it hard to get hold of.

The difficulty is trying to keep in view that in the 'here and now' of a promise or pledge or commitment to keep the future open, the future to come in a certain way arrives, arrives that is *as* the *now doing everything one can* to keep at bay what would always be a premature triumphal announcement of a *final arrival* – a final end of history – an arrival which would remain premature in any future present. And thus we might say that what Derrida always attempted to produce in any 'here and now' was a philosophical text-event that ought to remain at points essentially beyond the horizon of its own 'here and now'. It is a text that does not want to leave nothing to be desired, that positively welcomes the chance that it will not be consumed in the present or give itself up to an immediate understanding; that the text, and ourselves as readers of this text, remains ahead of us and to come.

I will return to the theme of democracy in Derrida in the penultimate chapter. For now, I want to take from this an indication of what it might mean to speak, as I would want to, of the *virtuosity* evident in Derrida's text.

Interrupting the straight talk which would have virtuosity thought of simply as the awesome 'know-how' of a master, the virtuosity of the Derridean philosophical text-event is a performance from him that cannot be reduced to performance by him; the event 'here and now' exceeds anything one might hope to appropriate as an expression, pure and simple, of '*his* power' or identify without qualification as '*his* performance'. As Derrida puts it in the last book he published during his lifetime, *Rogues*, 'a certain unconditional renunciation of sovereignty is required a priori'.

Interestingly, and I think plausibly, the structure in view here cannot be wholly stabilized in terms of the grammar of voluntary and intentional action. It is intentional all right (through and through), but it is an intentional act that does not exclude within itself (through and through) a 'letting happen' of something unforeseeable, something unanticipatable.

Though I do take Derrida to be a kind of virtuoso in this sense, I do not think he is unique in that regard. Anyone who has found themselves finding the right word or found themselves hitting a ball down a line or into the crowd or into the back of the net knows that even though it all happens through them, in utterly human form, what takes place is inadequately understood solely in terms of the deliberate effort of this 'human-one' to make some 'object-thing' or 'event-moment' happen. It happens, and *in the event* activity and passivity cannot be parsed out or rigorously distributed across the performance. It is both completely deliberate and yet came of itself. This does not mean one has to think of oneself as 'possessed', which would make the event merely a matter of taking something of the intentionality of another *in*; but nor can it be grasped completely as 'expression' either, which would make the event merely a matter of pushing something of one's own *out*. As we are beginning to see, the surprising theme, the theme which evidently surprised Derrida and gets Derrida's text moving, is one that has never been far from our thinking of the heights of human virtuosity: writing.

Chapter 4
The turn to writing

Derrida's special attention to writing as a theme for philosophy takes its point of departure from a gesture of *suspicion* concerning the status of writing that he regards as the 'philosophical movement *par excellence*', a gesture that one finds already in Plato's condemnation of writing in the *Phaedrus*, and hence taking in a heritage stretching back 'at least some twenty centuries'. On the other hand, however, this heritage is not a static order, and within the time of this philosophical movement *par excellence* Derrida identifies a shifting development which ultimately comes to a head when the attention of 'the most diverse researches' finally turned to *language*.

People often talk about a 'linguistic turn' today, meaning that intellectual inquiry in recent times has conceived its problems as fundamentally problems *about* language, or at least problems whose solution is fundamentally *dependent upon* a correct analysis of language. This 'turn' was, in Derrida's view, a very long time coming, and far from breaking with tradition or with metaphysics, it was, he thinks, in its innermost trajectory, its culmination; making visible, he claims, the deep structural configuration of the Western metaphysical tradition, neither completing it nor overcoming it.

Is Derrida part of this linguistic turn? Is his work a moment of it? In view of his emphasis on the need to 'make explicit the experience of language', it would seem that it is. Indeed, Derrida's writings are frequently regarded, and it would seem for good reason, as an extreme example of it. His claims that a work of reading 'cannot legitimately transgress the text towards something other than it', and (more notoriously) that 'there is nothing outside the text', are deeply suggestive of the idea that his work takes the linguistic turn, even outlines a form of linguistic idealism. For Derrida, the 'person writing' and everything that is normally treated as 'the real life of these existences "of flesh and bone"', is not, in his view, something 'beyond or behind' what we usually like to believe we can unproblematically circumscribe as 'so-and-so's text'. On the contrary, he insists that this 'real life' is itself something 'inscribed in a determined textual system'.

So it is all just language then.

If *that* was what Derrida was saying, he might even deserve the denunciations and smears to which he was so regularly treated. He would be guilty of an absurd *inflation* of language. If what Derrida appeals to, in the quotations cited above, as the 'textual system' were indeed a 'linguistic system', we could surely have been done with him long before he died. But it never was that, it most emphatically never was.

To begin to understand a formulation like 'there is nothing outside the text', we have first to acknowledge that the notion of 'the text' at work here does not relate to a system of language but, in a sense of 'writing' that I will explore and clarify in this chapter and the next, to *the structure of writing*. There is a traditional idea that spoken language is prior to writing, and we may feel this naturally ourselves. However, what we find in Derrida is a new way of thinking about this idea that deserves careful attention. For Derrida, language, and all that we think of as belonging to language – words, sentences, signs, speech, writing (in the usual sense), rules, meaning, reference, and so on – are made possible by, are 'opened by', and must ultimately be understood in terms of, the structure of writing (in his new sense): 'writing thus *comprehends* language'.

With this new conception in hand, Derrida's text, far from being part of a distinctively *linguistic* turn in philosophy, is actually striving to work beyond it, precisely to situate it. Indeed, as is emphasized at the start of the opening chapter of *Of Grammatology*, Derrida does not regard the current turn to language as *a methodological must* for a satisfactory and rigorous philosophy, but more like *a historical necessity* within the epoch we still inhabit. Moreover, for Derrida, this is an age whose old conceptuality is in increasing disrepair and which 'seems to be approaching what is really its own *exhaustion*'. As we shall see, with the appearance in various domains of a *graphematic turn* in our time (a turn towards writing) we are, Derrida claims, witnessing nothing less than 'a new mutation in the history of writing, in history as writing':

> However the topic is considered, the *problem of language* has never been simply one problem among others. But never as much as at present has it invaded, as such, the global horizon of the most diverse researches and the most heterogeneous discourses . . . The devaluation of the word 'language' itself, and how, in the very hold it has upon us, it betrays a loose vocabulary, the temptation of a cheap seduction, the passive yielding to fashion, the consciousness of the avant-garde, in other words – ignorance – are evidences of this effect. This inflation of the sign 'language' is the inflation of the sign itself, absolute inflation, inflation itself. Yet, by one of its aspects or shadows, it is itself still a sign: this crisis is also a symptom. It indicates, as if in spite of itself, that a historico-metaphysical epoch must finally determine as language the totality of its problematic horizon. It must do so . . . because . . . language itself is menaced in its very life . . . when it ceases to be self-assured, contained, and guaranteed by the infinite signified which seemed to exceed it.
>
> By a slow movement whose necessity is hardly perceptible, everything that for at least some twenty centuries tended toward,

> and finally succeeded in being gathered under, the name of language is beginning to let itself be transferred to, or at least summarized under the name of, writing.

This vast historical sweep, so confidently laid out in the opening pages to *Of Grammatology*, establishes an orientation from which Derrida's text never wavers. The abrupt hostility to the contemporary inflation of language and the sign, the so-called 'linguistic turn', is distinctive too. The widespread reach of that turn (which is, he suggests, more of a 'straight ahead' than a 'turn' in the historical movement of our heritage) is not regarded as a fertile philosophical advance but as a kind of cultural poverty, a movement which, far from being justified by clearly articulated reasons, is characterized by its 'loose vocabulary', 'cheap seduction', 'fashion', all in all a turn marked more by 'ignorance' than a powerful new theoretical advance. On the other hand, Derrida regards this historical movement in which the linguistic sign is pushed to the fore in so many domains of intellectual culture as itself a kind of sign or symptom: language comes to the centre in this way because everything that seemed solidly to render its status as essentially *un*problematic, everything that had assured us that it (language) *is* what we thought it *should* be; namely, the system of external or sensible signification of an order of pure intelligibility (meaning, ideality), an order traditionally grasped in terms of *the divine word* or *divine logos* (the 'infinite signified') has begun to melt into air.

One might well want to invoke Nietzsche's pronouncement that 'God is dead' to interpret the kind of disenchanting claim that Derrida is making against this enchanted conception of linguistic meaning. But I would rather recommend reading what Derrida has to say about the history of writing (and, indeed, history *as* writing), and his presentation of our time as witnessing the end of a certain idea of 'the book', as a new and powerful way of giving content to that rather heady slogan. Of course, the possibility of making sense of such a massive motif through the seemingly unremarkable and insignificant topic of writing can seem pretty extraordinary. But according to Derrida, there are systematic and irreducible links between, on the one hand, the conception of the sign through which, still today, we generally obtain our understanding of writing and, on the other hand, 'the epoch of Christian creationism . . . when these appropriate the resources of Greek conceptuality'.

Central to this linkage is the classical construal of linguistic signs as the unity of a (worldly) sensible signifier and an (ideal, mental, conceptual) intelligible signified. While this signified need not everywhere be related to the idea of the divine *logos* of a creator God, as the 'pure face of intelligibility' it is still immediately caught up with the idea of the *logos* in general, caught up with the idea of an order of pure intelligibility. And this idea simply cannot be 'innocently separated' from its 'metaphysical-theological roots' in the thought of the divine *logos* which, it is written, is the being-there of God 'in the beginning': ultimately inseparable from the idea of the 'word or face' of God. According to Derrida, then, 'the sign and divinity have the same place and time of birth. The age of the sign is essentially theological.' And, in such an age, *writing*, the very image of the worldly or sensible signifier *essentially* exterior to the *logos* as pure intelligibility, can only find itself 'debased'.

If it is writing and not language that is now beginning to impose itself as the gathering point for thought and research, then the heading of 'Man' may be undergoing an epochal shift: the fundamental structures of human life and history will be conceived otherwise than in terms of the 'Greek conceptuality' of the *zōon logon echon* [the living thing with the capacity for *logos*, fatefully translated into the Latin of the Roman Republic as *animal rationale*] or of the 'Christian creationism' of the theomorphic *ens creatum*. The traditional discourse of human history, the discourse of Man, the rational animal, taking itself home on a linear journey towards his proper end, may be on its last legs.

While Derrida's reassessment of writing is bound up with an effort to liberate our understanding of it from the Greco-Christian or onto-theological system of evaluative assessment in which it still remains, he also recognizes that, in fact, writing has not always been condemned to a kind of fallen secondariness. Within the age of the sign, there is (as one might have suspected) 'good' as well as 'bad' writing. However, what is at issue with such good writing has always been an essentially *figurative* or metaphorical sense of writing again immediately connected with the divine *logos* (especially evident in the premodern idea of 'the book of Nature' that would be 'God's writing'), a sense of writing which precisely *defines* (and note the interesting inversion of the usual order of priority between the figurative and the literal here) the *literal* meaning as a 'merely human' tool in the sensible world: writing as one of Man's technical instruments is the secondary supplement to speech, speech appearing here as the more ethereal (and in so-called 'inner speech', itself fundamentally *non-exterior*) and natural *first* signifier. Worldly writing, what has always been identified as 'the signifier of the signifier', is just a mark, a trace, and has nothing to do with (or can only threaten to contaminate) the pure life and proper development of spirit; it has nothing to do with any good writing that it is the task of literate civilized men to study and learn:

> The good writing has therefore always been *comprehended*. Comprehended as that which had to be comprehended: within a nature or a natural law, created or not, but first thought within an eternal presence. Comprehended, therefore, within a totality, and enveloped in a volume or a book. The idea of the book is the idea of a totality, finite or infinite, of the signifier; this totality of the signifier cannot be a totality, unless a totality constituted by the signified pre-exists it, supervises its inscriptions and its signs, and is independent of it in its ideality . . . If I distinguish the text from the book, I shall say that the destruction of the book, as it is now under way in all domains, denudes the surface of the text.

This motif of the 'end of the book' is not a prediction that libraries will start closing down, but a figure for a situation which we have, in a certain way, always already known is our own but which today is 'in the process of making itself known *as such*'. The classic conception of a *logos*, or good writing, that would be an ideal presence, a pre-existing and occult (that is, hidden) 'realm of spirit' – an order of pure intelligibility in principle graspable by Man as a 'spiritual' being – beyond what is denounced as bad (because wholly worldly and exterior) writing, that conception is, in our today, increasingly unbelievable. 'Man', and the *logos*-centred order through which 'Man' has been understood, is no longer in good shape.

Equally, however, what is in the process of making itself known as such today is that everything that has been situated as *external* to (and hence what has threatened to contaminate) what has been regarded as the life proper to Man (for example, the order of marks, tracks, and traces, concepts non-accidentally connected to – supposedly – 'merely animal' existence) is the very condition of possibility of that life. Indeed, if 'writing' covers the formation of marks and traces in general, then, one might say that 'there is no linguistic sign before writing'. As we shall see in greater detail in the next chapter, the affirmation in Derrida's text of a renewed understanding of 'writing' as both preceding and exceeding 'the letter' (and indeed language in general) is not an affirmation of what is traditionally regarded as bad writing any more than it is an endorsement of its metaphorical other. Derrida's pronouncement of a turn in our time marked by the 'destruction of the book' is, like Nietzsche's pronouncement of 'the death of God', neither a brutal materialism, nor a hopeless nihilism, nor, indeed, despite appearances, an 'atheist critique' of religious belief. Rather, it is an attempt to articulate the movement already underway within our epoch. It is part of an effort to read our time, inviting us to re-think our understanding of the world and the significance of our lives. It invites us to re-look at the movement of the history of philosophy as the logocentric epoch in deconstruction.

On the other hand, the rehabilitation of writing leaves us with no way of giving content to the idea of *criticising* or *critically assessing* anything that does, for a participant, give life a meaning in terms of attaining a "truth" that is already "written" (for example, in some kind of good writing we might intuit or have revealed to us) "outside the text". That kind of reassuring *cognitivism* – the idea that there is something to be *known* in this matter – is not to be had, and never was even when "Western man" lived a life which firmly presumed it was.

This is, without doubt, an extraordinary radicalization and acceleration of the modern, Enlightenment critique of enchanted nature and of the *logos* as pure order of intelligibility. And one can readily see why the authors who Derrida finds most compelling are those who have most powerfully questioned the fundamental transcendentalism, supernaturalism, and the ethnocentrism of Western *logos*-centred thinking – Rousseau, Marx, Nietzsche, Freud, Saussure, Husserl, Heidegger, Levinas, J. L. Austin. Some strange bedfellows here, and each can and will be criticized by Derrida for falling short in some respects, for repeating gestures rooted in the very heritage they also criticize. However, for Derrida, these thinkers do not stand *squarely* within the logocentrism of the Greco-Christian epoch, and their importance resides in the power of their work to call into question its onto-theological roots.

As I have already indicated, this is not to say that Derrida regards himself as one who would want simply to 'reject' these roots. Indeed, we have our being in this heritage and so any putative breakthrough which would hope genuinely to '*criticize* metaphysics radically' must (can only) make (inventive) use of the resources of the heritage we actually inhabit: there is no claim to a critique from outside here. And for Derrida, the fundamental lever of this radical criticism of metaphysics will be provided by the re-evaluation of that seemingly harmless and hitherto hardly philosophically central or philosophically unavoidable concept of writing.

According to Derrida, then, the so-called linguistic turn is not just an event (happy or not) which happened to take place not so long ago. On the contrary, he regards the emergence of the problem of language as belonging profoundly to the history of Western metaphysics in its internal development. However, the movement of that history is also characterized by the ever more radical questioning of and uncertainty regarding the onto-theological presuppositions of traditional Western thought, and Derrida belongs to that general movement of 'enlightenment' too. Nevertheless, what Derrida perceives in the modern focus on language and on the linguistic sign as a two-sided unity of a phonetic signifier and signified meaning, is not fertile ground for further rational and scientific critiques of premodern superstition but an inconspicuous and essentially dogmatic retention of fundamental motifs of the very onto-theological tradition that it typically regards itself as overcoming. The idea of the sign: the most surreptitious and perhaps last stand of the logocentric epoch.

On the basis of a 'theoretical matrix' that presents the age of the sign as everywhere caught up in a metaphysics of *phonetic* writing, Derrida will himself make a stand against the modern inflation of the sign 'language'. And as I have indicated, what he finds most significant, radical, and interesting is not the so-called *linguistic turn* but signs of a growing *graphematic turn* in the historical tide. For some time now, people have said 'language for action, movement, thought, reflection, consciousness, unconsciousness, experience, affectivity etc.'. Today, however, Derrida suggests, 'we tend to say "writing" for all that and more':

> to designate not only the physical gestures of literal pictographic or ideographic inscription, but also the totality of what makes it possible; and also, beyond the signifying face, the signified face itself. And thus we say 'writing' for all that gives rise to an inscription in general, whether it is literal or not and even if what it distributes in space is alien to the order of the voice: cinematography, choreography, of course, but also pictorial, musical, sculptural

> 'writing'. One might also speak of athletic writing, and with even greater certainty of military or political writing in view of the techniques that govern those domains today. All this to describe not only the system of notation secondarily connected with these activities but the essence and content of these activities themselves. It is also in this sense that the contemporary biologist speaks of writing and *pro-gram* in relation to the most elementary processes of information within the living cell. And, finally, whether it has essential limits or not, the entire field covered by the cybernetic program will be the field of writing. If the theory of cybernetics is by itself to oust all metaphysical concepts – including the concepts of soul, of life, of value, of choice, of memory – which until recently served to separate the machine from man, it must conserve the notion of writing, trace, *grammè* [written mark], or *grapheme*, until its own historico-metaphysical character is also exposed.

Supposing this is indeed the way things are going, and it seems to me clear that it is even more obvious than it was in 1967 that 'we tend to say' today writing-related rather than language-related things when we reach for an articulation of deep structures of human life: it is, we tend to say today, in the 'code' of our DNA, written in our genes, traces in the brain, and so on. The metaphors and similes are often biological but they are also often machinic. Today, computer analogies are ubiquitous. Computers 'run' a 'program', and they do so (once programmed) without an assumption of a runner, without a 'who' which is behind the written code, a presence behind or accompanying the unimaginably rapid sequences of 1s and 0s.

Of course, these are pre-theoretical tendencies of our time – and, one might want to insist, to make a computer you still need a programmer who is a who and not a machine. On the other hand, this is the question today: how like a machine, how embedded within programs, within machination, both biological and cultural, is the life of a human being? And does this altogether exclude what we do not want to exclude: responsibility, chance, decision, the unanticipatable event? Derrida thinks not. We will come back to this.

In any case, since it is a pre-theoretical tendency, why should we take the idea of a 'graphematic turn' any more seriously or regard it as more significant than the so-called 'linguistic turn'? Of course, I have already begun to suggest why a graphematic turn may have profound historico-metaphysical implications. But Derrida knows that unless he offers an 'attempt to justify it', his involvement in this turn within the history of (or as) writing, will be guilty of precisely 'giving in to the movement of inflation' which he had denounced so trenchantly in the so-called linguistic turn. So what could possibly justify it? What is it about writing, if anything, which makes it fit to be the gathering point for so many developments taking place today? In the next two chapters, I will outline the way I have come to see the shape of Derrida's argumentative justification for engaging in the graphematic turn, the fundamentals of the 'theoretical matrix' that shape the development of a new grammatological opening in thought.

Art Center College of Design
Library
1700 Lida Street
Pasadena, Calif. 91103

Chapter 5
Différance

In the age of the sign which we still inhabit, the philosophical ambition of becoming 'completely clear' is conceived as a matter of overcoming difficulties by achieving the *complete disambiguation of what we mean, that is to say, of the signified.* Or, as one might better put it after Derrida, overcoming difficulties through *the reduction of dissemination* (the idea of countless sense-making paths, introduced in Chapter 2) *to polysemia* (the idea of a countable number of distinct senses). The point, the traditional philosopher might want to say, is not the signifier or word, whether written or spoken, but the *meaning* – the *logos* – which we grasp in a flash when we hear and understand a word. And what we grasp here, in grasping a sense, must be something that is, in a fundamental way, single and identifiable: a meaning that *is* one, the traditional philosopher might say, must be a meaning that is *one*.

Derrida's text sets itself the task of thinking the identity in question here without giving in to this urge to reduce dissemination to polysemia, indeed to 'oppose' them. And along with that new task, we find also a change in ambition for an heir to the subject that was called 'philosophy'. The task is no longer to achieve superlative conceptual clarity in the sense of rendering what we mean perfectly transparent in its identity, but rather to learn how to endure reflectively what we already more or less naively endure every day, indeed as our everyday itself; our inhabitation of a fundamentally 'inscriptural space', a text, marked by an irreducible (which is not to say simply unlimited) *play* within identity that Derrida will formalize in terms of a new (but recognizably still French) word '*différance*' (with an a). Philosophy, as the desire to reduce dissemination, takes place as the impossible project to eliminate this play. Commenting on a passage from Aristotle, Derrida offers the following summary of what we might call *the* philosophical conception of language:

> A noun [for Aristotle] is proper when it has but a single sense. Better, it is only in this case that it is properly a noun. Univocity is the essence, or better, the *telos* of language. No philosophy, as such, has ever renounced this Aristotelian ideal. This ideal is philosophy . . . Each time that polysemia is irreducible, when no unity of meaning is even promised to it, one is [according to philosophy] outside language. And consequently outside humanity.

The link between what is proper for language and a conception of what is proper for Man is something I have already touched upon and will take up again in the final chapter of this book. However, it will be helpful to anticipate at this point that the idea according to which we understand the human as 'the speaking being' (in a sense appropriate to the Aristotelian ideal of language), and indeed the *only* such speaking being, is regarded by Derrida as highly problematic. Moreover, the account of language he will provide in turn will enable him strongly to 'contest [the view] that [the conditions of possibility of a language] give rise to a single linear, indivisible, oppositional limit, to a binary opposition between the human and the non-human'. As we shall see, against this kind of binary or oppositional conception he will not affirm a kind of biological 'continuism'. On the contrary, he does not want to deny the specificity or distinctive 'originality' to the structures of life that belong to different living things, including living human beings, at all. However, he does want to insist that these distinctive differences are misconceived if they are construed, as philosophy has always tended to do, such that it is 'always a matter of marking an absolute limit' between human beings and other animals, as if the significance we attach to the idea of the difference between human beings and other animals (a significance Derrida will insist upon and not reduce) was grounded in an appreciation of how things objectively are. Central to such a thought would be the idea that human beings, uniquely, are 'speaking creatures', and that this capacity for language is the mark of a radical break or cut-off point between such a creature and every other (merely or purely) living thing. But Derrida resists the idea that the significance we attach to the idea of the difference between human beings and other animals has this kind of objectivity. As he puts it, 'human language, as original as it might be, does not allow us to "cut" once and for all where we would in general like to cut'. The supposed uniqueness and 'dignity' of the human, if it is to be affirmed at all, will no longer be thinkable in terms of a radical separation from animal life of this kind.

It will bear repeating that Derrida's effort to make problematic the traditional Aristotelian – or let's say simply philosophical – conception of language does not mean that he wants simply to affirm the opposite, that plurivocity or polysemia is the essence, or the *telos*, of language. The intention to oppose polysemia with dissemination does not aim to affirm that everything we say is ambiguous (that every word is characterized by at least two or more meanings), but that polysemia is *irreducible* in the sense that *each and every* 'meaning' is itself subject, as we saw in Chapter 2, to more than one understanding.

Thus, when it comes to thinking about the *identity* of an expression, Derrida does not deny the necessity or propriety of talking about a minimum idealization, the possibility of identifying an expression as *the same again* in a new situation, or in a new context. However, and this will bring us to one of Derrida's most constant themes, he insists that the sorts of *differences* in our understanding of an expression that arise from our sensitivity or receptivity to its interpretative context are not finally separable from the *identity* of the expression that we recognize and know how to use. And it is not that 'understanding an expression' has two different meanings (this would be 'polysemia' again): one capturing, say, 'knowing how it is used' (mastery of the machine), the other 'knowing what it is about' (sensitivity to a context). It is that both these kinds of use of 'understanding' (where we say that what is understood is 'the same' as in some other context, and where we say what is understood is unreplaceably singular and 'different' from other contexts), as Wittgenstein puts it, 'make up my *concept* of understanding'. They are in play on the multitude of paths we take with this word, 'for I *want* to apply the word "understanding" to all this'.

This idea, the thought of a logic of understanding marked by both identity and difference, is complex and worth careful elucidation. In this chapter and the next, I will focus exclusively on what I take to be Derrida's most effective demonstrations and arguments in relation to this theme. Some of this will involve a rather advanced level of discussion, and will be formalizing Derrida's ideas as much as merely introducing them or providing a commentary on them. Nevertheless, given that Derrida has been subject to so much abuse as a thinker, it is important to see how his rehabilitation of writing is supported by step-by-step arguments of various sorts. His work in this area is, in my view, both interesting and compelling, and I want to make an effort to show up the rigour within a text that might otherwise seem wilfully obscure.

Discriminating differences

In Chapter 2, I introduced Derrida's affirmation of dissemination in terms of the non-reducible plurality of *different* understandings of the *same* text. This conception of differences-within-the-same identity is not simply affirmed in Derrida's work, it is thematized, described, and, as far as possible, formalized. In many of his texts, we are invited to understand this feature in terms of what he calls the movement of '*différance*' that marks the structure and functioning of every signifying form. It is his commitment to thinking about all identities in terms of this movement that can make it so difficult to work out what he means. Or, as he puts it himself, it is what he invites us to think in terms of this movement that 'makes the thinking of it uneasy and uncomfortable'.

As a prelude to introducing this idea, and the value of identity-in-*différance* that is developed in Derrida's text, I will first provide a formalized version of why, according to Derrida, we are obliged to go beyond traditional philosophical resources for thinking about the discrimination of the identity of signs; namely, in terms of one or other of two distinctively human receptive faculties, faculties corresponding to the two sides of the sign as classically understood: sensibility and understanding.

The first steps are as follows.

1. Assume that what belongs to sensibility are always perceptions of some present sensory data. (For example, assume that what can be 'heard' is always 'a sound or is composed of sounds or properties of sounds'.)
2. Articulate, meaningful speech is, by definition, something which can be heard.
3. For articulate, meaningful speech to be possible, a language must contain a number of discriminably different 'units' (call them 'phonemes'). People must be able to discriminate different phonemes if speech is to function as such.
4. The *difference* between two phonemes is not itself a sound – not some third sound, not an audible 'something'.
5. Therefore the difference which establishes speech and lets it be heard is inaudible (in every sensory sense of the word).
6. But since meaningful speech is possible, the difference between two phonemes must still be discriminable.
7. Therefore, one ought to reject the idea that such discrimination belongs to sensibility.

What is discriminated when one hears an identifiable phoneme *cannot* be reduced to a sound which is simply present in the present. And hence we need to reject the first premise of the argument: *what is heard* is not reducible to sounds or properties of sounds, something fully present in the present. At this point, Derrida affirms something of the *differential* conception of signs proposed by structuralist linguistics, according to which 'identity can only determine or delimit itself through differential relations to other elements'.

The steps we have just run through capture the part of Derrida's discussion in his essay 'Différance' that relates to a rejection of the assumption that an adequate account of the discrimination of phonemes 'belongs to sensibility' (i.e. can be understood in terms of what is simply given as 'present to the senses'). He then invites the repetition of the same argument for writing. Graphic differences 'can never be sensed as a full term' either. In short, in neither case can we maintain the view that the discrimination of differences which makes possible the apprehension of linguistic signs 'belongs to sensibility'.

In the very next sentence, Derrida goes on to claim that it cannot belong to an order of intelligibility either (i.e. cannot be understood as something discriminated by the understanding as that is construed by philosophy). We cannot conclude, as for example Descartes might have concluded, that what is at issue here is something that is present to, and that is 'seen' or 'heard' by, the mind's eye/ear.

This step in Derrida's argument draws in part from a wider recognition that human understanding has been interpreted, from Greek times, in terms derived from sensibility, or perhaps better, it draws on the fact that from Greek times sensibility and understanding (perception and conception) have been *the* terms through which the principal faculties of human cognition have been interpreted, and *both* are interpreted in terms of the apprehension of something present – in terms, that is, of the same 'logic of presence'. It is this 'logic' that, Derrida is arguing here, the differential structure of signs resists or escapes. And so we can now add to (7) the following parallel conclusion:

8. Therefore, one ought to reject the idea that such discrimination belongs to intelligibility.

At which point, we reach a devastating final dialectical blow:

9. We must let ourselves refer to an order that resists one of the founding oppositions of philosophy.

This order 'is announced', Derrida says, 'in a movement of *différance* . . . which belongs neither to the voice nor to writing in the usual sense'.

The idea of a 'movement of *différance*' is, I think, best understood as working to subvert and replace a tempting and deeply intuitive conception of *identity* and *difference* (with an e), a particular conception of *what makes something what it is and different to another thing*.

Everything has an identity, and this identity is what distinguishes or makes it different from everything else; it is what makes it what it is (a cough, a chair, a cup, a rainbow, a Venetian princess, the King of France, the word 'blue', the meaning of the word 'rogue') and not another thing. How should we understand the logic of identity? Perhaps the most intuitive way of construing identity is in terms of the possession of distinguishing features. However, if the features determine identity then anything will be what it is only so long as it retains these features. The metaphysics of identity thus seems to require that a thing has the identity it does only as long as it *endures in presence* as the same. What makes anything the thing that it is rather than some other thing, what makes it, in some way or other, different from everything that it is not, is its possession of an identity that persists as the same as long as it is the thing that it is. This is a matter of its being as it is by way of *maintaining* its identity. On this view, when we say that something exists or comes into being, the meaning of its 'is' is its remaining or persisting in presence as the same.

Of course, for many things or kinds of thing, 'retaining its identity' is compatible with a certain amount of change. However, if one adheres to the intuitive metaphysics of identity just outlined, one is likely to think that certain changes will simply be too fundamental, and that what once was will no longer be or ceases to be or has become something else if such radical changes take place. One may or may not suppose that there are 'essential' features or 'defining' features, which were a thing to lack them it would necessarily cease to be what it was, but the crucial idea is nevertheless that 'being a such and such' (rather than a something else) must be understood on the basis of some kind of persisting presence. Whether such things are supposed real or ideal is not to the point; what matters is that, when and for as long as it is, *it* must remain present in and of itself as the same.

What persists in its identity in this way can be given one of two interpretations: the identity at issue may be construed as either *intrinsic* or *relational*. On the first construal, it is the presence of certain features that makes a thing the thing that it is: a thing would not continue to be the self-same-thing if *it* (which has them) lost them, or enough of them. On the other hand, on this construal, as far as the identity of anything is concerned, what the rest of the universe is like is more or less irrelevant – there may even be, as a matter of fact, other things which have the self-same features, and then the only distinction between them – if they are indeed different – is quantitative: there is more than one of them persisting in presence.

On the second construal, by contrast, the difference to other things is internal to a thing's identity, so that something is what it is in virtue of its occupying a particular position in a structure of general differentiation: anything that is a specific something or other (rather something else) persists in presence as itself only in terms of the persisting in presence of that structure of general differentiation. Whether this structure is regarded as real or ideal is again not to the point; what matters is that, when and for as long as the structure of differentiation is as it is, *it* remains, as we might put it, present in and of itself as the same.

Derrida's counter-conception of identity is different from both of these, although, as I have already indicated, he shares the emphasis of the second view on the idea that identity is differentially constituted or constructed in a relational way. Derrida's counter-conception, however, is that when it comes to such constructed identities, what makes something what it is and not another thing (what gives it the identity it has) is *not* (merely) a matter of its relationships of difference to *other* things within a general schema or structure of general differentiation but a matter of what he calls a *self-difference*, a *difference to itself*. On this very counter-intuitive counter-conception of identity a certain non-self-sameness is internal to every constructed identity. That is, the 'otherness' that is implied in every identity is not 'the other that it is not' but a certain otherness within itself, *the other in the same*. According to *this new Derridean manner of speaking*, every identity has an irreducibly 'divided identity', is characterized by a 'difference with itself', or an 'originary alienation'.

As I say, this conception endorses something of the idea that identity emerges from a system of differences (with an e). However, what that (let's call it) structuralist construal fails sufficiently to acknowledge is that such systems of differences do not 'fall from the sky' ready-made or fully formed but themselves come to be. Derrida's question is: is the movement through which the system of general differentiation comes to be, itself something that is in some sense *present*? Supposing the existence of such a system is the condition of identity, we might well wonder whether the movement that brings such a system into being is something that can itself appear 'on the stage of presence' as such. One possibility here would be to present or represent this movement as, simply, *the movement of differentiation*. The problem is, however, that this implies a process in which some kind of substantial something or other *gets differentiated*. But the only 'prior' presence in this case is itself a system of differentiation.

The father of structuralist linguistics, Ferdinand de Saussure, had a proposal to deal with this problem that Derrida considers both helpful and ultimately unacceptable. Saussure's proposal is that we can find an origin of differentiation by focusing on the system *in operation*, in *speech*:

> Language is necessary in order for speech to be intelligible and to produce all its effects; but the latter is necessary in order for language to be established; historically, the fact of speech always comes first.

In the essay 'Différance', Derrida provisionally accepts something like this account of language as valid for 'the sign in general', and for every 'code' or 'system of referral in general': what Derrida calls '*différance*' can be understood as the movement through which every sign 'is constituted historically as a weave of differences'. However, he also admits that the account given by Saussure appears to enclose us in a 'circle', and is not in its own terms satisfactory. The replacement of 'speech' by '*différance*' in the Saussurean formula of the 'origin' of the system is an effort to confront this problem.

In Derrida's view, an analysis of language which begins with a radical distinction between the 'system' (Saussure's *langue* as language *qua* system of rules) and the 'event' (Saussure's *parole* as language *qua* event of speech) necessarily deprives itself of the means with which to provide an account of the possibility of the very phenomenon it is claiming to delimit. This is because the impossible combination of both the historical priority and the logical posteriority of speech ruins any attempt to provide an internally consistent account of the conditions of possibility for the phenomenon of language. As Derrida puts it:

> If one rigorously distinguishes *langue* and *parole*, code and message, schema and usage, etc., and if one wishes to do justice to the two postulates thus enunciated, one does not know where to begin, or how something can begin in general, be it language or speech.

The claim here is not that the Saussurean circle is vicious in the sense of being a proof which presupposes that which requires demonstration. Rather, it is a 'chicken and egg' difficulty: 'one does not know where to begin'. Thus, Saussure is not really justified in appealing to the historical priority of speech. For 'speech' (*parole*) must be opposed to mere babble, or mere noise production, and this is possible, on Saussure's account, only if 'language' (*langue*) is present. Hence, as soon as one rigorously distinguishes the system from the event of language, these concepts become 'unreliable' when one is concerned with questions concerning the conditions of the possibility for speech or writing to be understandable, or comprehended in general. And this is Derrida's principal concern.

This point can be made in another way by conceiving the circle in the form of a regress. As we have seen, if one works within the schema of the Saussurean distinction, the system of rules is conceived as fixing the sense of words across variations of context of speech. However, if these rules are acknowledged as having a normative role in the use of signs, then it seems clear that among the 'events of speech' we must be able to identify 'expressions of rules'. However, on the model under examination, if such 'expressions of rules' are to be intelligible, then they must be governed by rules, rules which must, if they are to function as such, be expressible . . . and so on.

Derrida does not think that circularity or regress is inevitable here. Rather, treating it as a *reductio ad absurdum* (a reduction to absurdity) of any attempt to determine the conditions of possibility of the functioning of speech and writing on the basis of a radical system/event or code/message distinction, he concludes that such problems show the necessity of accounting for this functioning in terms which do not begin by splitting things up in this way. If we are to overcome the 'chicken and egg' oscillation, what is needed, therefore, is a way of 'thinking at once both the rule and the event'.

It is for this reason that Derrida eschews recourse to the concept of the code or system of rules in an account of the discrimination of signs, and refers instead to *the movement that produces the system of differences* – the condition of possibility of all lexical and conceptual identities – by the neologism or neographism '*différance*' (with an a).

So the basic effort is an attempt to shift us away from thinking that – whether we are thinking about the discrimination of a 'word' or 'the meaning of a word'– we are concerned with something that might ever be simply or fully 'present in and of itself'. Remember, we are in the zone of a critique of a quite specific metaphysics of identity here, and there is no question of denying that 'elements of signification' – the 'substance' of language, if you like – have some kind of discriminable identity. What is being denied is that this can be construed in terms of the discrimination (by the ear or eye or by the mind's ear or eye) of a persisting presence. That there is some kind of identity at issue is simply undeniable – we say that 'this is *the same* word as that one, it is just badly written', and we say that different people or one person at different times are 'working with *the same* concepts'. However, it is equally clear that identity in these cases always 'defers to its interpretative context'. In other words, it belongs to what is recognized as 'present here and now', that *it* can persist as *the same* in and through 'repetitions' that involve *different* interpretive contexts.

It is with this intertwining of difference-within-identity or the-other-within-the-same that the Derridean idea of an identity that includes a certain 'difference to itself' takes shape. It is just this dimension of *difference-within-identity* that Derrida wants to get into view with his term '*différance*' (with an a). Of course, the French word '*différence*' (with an e) already brings into view the semantic dimension of, precisely, *difference*. Derrida appeals to a second sense belonging to the Latin verb '*differre*' but completely absent from the French '*différence*' that was in fact derived from it; namely, 'the action of putting off' – deferring. The point here is to get a semantic dimension of *sameness* into play as well (and into play *without* a commitment to a deferred *presence*; the only essential thing at issue when someone defers doing something is that instead of doing x now, they intend to do x later – whether 'doing x' can escape the logic of identity-in-différance being elaborated is a further question). French '*différence*' (with an e) does not have this semantic component. Thence the value of a neologism which will compensate for this lack, with a term with greater semantic wealth: 'we provisionally give the name *différance* to this sameness which is not identical'.

Within this new Derridean (French-ish) *manner of speaking*, we can say that it is because there is, in the case of elements of signification, no identity without *différance* (with an a) that we can affirm that, an ordinary *différence* (with an e) is always a *différence* (with an e) between elements whose own identity is always already marked by *différance* (with an a).

Without wishing to encourage the reader to indulge in an embarrassing French (spoken) accent, it is important to note that when you read the previous sentence you should not pronounce *différence* differently to *différance*. Not at all. Don't try to stretch out the 'a' in some kind of absurd pastiche of Franglais, for example. The two words are *intended* to be 'to the ear' perfectly indistinguishable, totally indiscriminable. So *say* them the same. The difference between them is, that is, exclusively 'graphic'.

Of course, the discriminable difference between two graphemes is no more (or, in the end, no less) visual than the discriminable difference between two phonemes is aural. As we have seen, graphic differences 'can never be sensed as a full term' any more than phonetic ones. So why retain this name? There is a very short argument here, and a longer one. The short argument, which we encountered in the last chapter, is nicely presented by Geoffrey Bennington like this:

> Derrida explains that he keeps to the term [writing] because writing was always determined as the signifier of a signifier; that's what he argues all signifiers are, and that's why he retains the term.

In the next chapter, I will outline the longer one, the argument in which the appeal to 'writing' finds its most radical justification: the argument from iterability. As we shall see, this will bring us back to the short argument, or at least to an enriched sense of its significance.

Chapter 6
Iterability

We have now reached what might be called *the first conclusion* of Derrida's text: 'the logic of presence' must be displaced, indeed will always already find itself destined to be displaced by the logic of *différance*. This logic is held to be in some way already known (although not known as such) in the classic philosophical assessment of what we call 'writing'. It is for this reason that a strategic borrowing of this old word occurs in an analysis which gives it a somewhat fresh sense. In this chapter, I will offer a reconstruction of this analysis.

What we might call Derrida's master argument for retaining the word 'writing' purports to show that 'the traits which can be recognized in the classical, narrowly defined concept of writing' are *necessarily valid* for all signs. While this claim to generality does not, for this reason, straightforwardly change or challenge the usual meaning of the word 'writing', it does put pressure on what we are inclined to say when we are asked about writing, and indeed what we are inclined to say about words of a language in general, as well as marks and traces beyond the human use of language.

What, then, is the classical, narrowly defined concept of 'writing'? According to Derrida, the classic philosophical conception regards writing as, first and foremost, a means of communication and, indeed, 'an especially potent means of communication'. What is the potency that is supposed to be so specific to writing? On the classical interpretation that Derrida wants to interrogate, writing emerges as a technical device when the desire or need arises to extend the field of communication to addressees who are present but who are out of range of the natural voice. Writing thus first appears *in fact* when the space of sociality has changed to the point when we need or want to send messages to others who are 'not only distant but outside of the entire field of vision and beyond earshot'.

In his first challenge to this classic construal, Derrida asks whether in fact and in principle this distance 'must be capable of being carried to a certain absoluteness of absence' if writing is to be possible. The question is then: is the absence of the addressee that is supposed to *specify* writing to be characterized in terms only of the distant presence of a receiver, or should the scope of this concept of absence be widened to include, at the limit, the possibility of the addressee's absolute absence – specifically, his or her death?

I write a letter and address it with a proper name. To do this is to write to an empirically determinable receiver or addressee. Of course, it is always possible that before receiving my written message, this addressee or these addressees may die. Does this prevent my writing from being read? Of course not. However, Derrida does not want the obviousness of this point to be taken to reflect a common-sense supplement to the classic view of writing. On the contrary, with the re-evaluation of the relationship of writing to absence, Derrida wants radically to transform the conceptual economy in this area. I will explain this.

Note first of all that the classic interpretation of writing does not mention the absence of the producer of the written mark who sends it away to be read elsewhere. It is clear, however, that parallel considerations must hold here too:

> To write is to produce a mark . . . which my future disappearance will not in principle, hinder in its functioning. . . . For a writing to be a writing it must continue to 'act' and to be readable even when what is called the author of the writing no longer answers for what he has written. . . . The situation of the writer is, concerning the written text, basically the same as that of the reader.

Derrida is not concerned here with writing or death only as empirical phenomena. Rather, his concern is with the logical possibility and not merely the physical opportunity for a written text to remain readable when the absence of the sender or the addressee is no longer a mode of presence but a radical or absolute absence. And his claim is that the possibility of it functioning again beyond (or in the absence of) the 'living present' of its context of production or its empirically determined destination is part of what it is to *be* a written mark: to be what it is, all writing must be capable of functioning beyond the death of *any* (although of course not *every*) empirically determinable user in general. We can thus propose the following 'law of writing': a mark that is not structurally readable – iterable – beyond the death of the empirically determinable producer and receiver would not be writing.

The general claim, then, is that the *possibility* of 'functioning in the absence of' implied by the classic conception of writing must be capable of being brought to an *absolute* limit if writing is to constitute itself as such. Any particular event of writing or reading, if it is to take place as such in any 'here and now', presumes as its condition of possibility the possibility of an iteration in the radical absence of this one.

So: any written message is readable only to the extent that a reader can read whatever a (determinable) sender could write in the radical absence of that sender: *writing can and must be able to do without the presence of the (determinable) sender*. Equally, any message is readable only to the extent that a (determinable) reader can read whatever the sender could write in the absolute absence of the (destined) receiver's presence: *writing can and must be able to do without the presence of the (destined) receiver.*

These two possible absences 'construct the possibility of the message itself'. That is, and *pace* the classic interpretation, it is not the relative permanence of the written word (its relatively continuous presence in being) which makes iterations possible in the absence of the sender (who is still present 'over here') or receiver (who is still present 'over there'); rather, the written mark is precisely made to make up for these *possible absences*.

It is with this conclusion that the idea of a strategic generalization of the term 'writing' becomes forceful. According to Derrida's argument, the absence that characterizes writing is not a function of the fact of its relative persistence or permanence but of logically necessary preconditions of its status *as* readable writing. It is true that these preconditions are most perspicuous in the case of writing, but what if these possibilities of absence can be acknowledged to be part of the structure of *every* 'event of communication', no matter of what kind, whatever the species?

The idea here is that a 'singular event' that functions as a means of communication (e.g. an event of speech) can be the event it is only on condition of a necessary or structural relation to an iteration that is *another such* singular event which is *not present* at the time of its production or reception, another event which is not what it is except in its relation to another such event, another such event which is not what it is except in relation to another such event. Although the movement is without limit, numbers are not accumulating here. Or rather, the limit is: *not once*. This is what Derrida is insisting upon when he states that the 'unity of the signifying form' that is 'required to permit its recognition' 'only constitutes itself by virtue of its iterability'. There are two major points to bring out here. First, it goes along with this thought that for a word *to be* at all is for it *to be used*. Second, and subsequently, it brings into prominence that the possibility of a written mark functioning *again* in the absence of the current presence of its user or its current context of use is not just a supplementary benefit of writing, but internal to its *being* the 'writing' it is – *no matter of what kind.*

In every case, an event of writing (no matter what kind) thus breaks away from its determinable author or producer. *What* I *do* now must, in its iterability, be sufficiently detachable from what *I* do *now* for it to *be* the writing it is in any 'here and now'.

In the essay in which this argument is most systematically developed, *Limited Inc*, Derrida takes up a potential counter-example. In fact, the counter-example is from the philosopher John Searle, who was responding to Derrida's argument from iterability as stated in 'Signature Event Context'. The counter-example is of a shopping list, something that can function, Searle supposes, in the presence of its recipient and without any relation to its absence ('for example, when I compose a shopping list for myself'). In what could be read as the beginning of a commentary on the first paragraph of Wittgenstein's *Philosophical Investigations*, Derrida remarks:

> *At the very moment* 'I' make a shopping list, I know (I use 'knowing' here as a convenient term to designate the relations that I necessarily entertain with the object being constructed) that it will only be a list if it implies my absence, if it already detaches itself from me in order to function beyond my 'present' act and if it is utilizable at another time, in the absence of my-being-present-now.

The factually late emergence of what we usually call 'writing', the eventual emergence of the use of a mark that can do without the current presence of a determinable sender or recipient, should not mislead us here. For that emergence is *possible* because, in principle, the possibility of this absence is part of the logical structure of *any* sign, linguistic or not, human or not, in general;

part of the conditions of possibility of any 'means of communication' in general. And this is why we might speak, as Derrida does, of a 'writing before the letter' that makes what we normally call 'the written letter' possible. Hence, according to Derrida, the point is that language must be grasped as 'a possibility founded on the general possibility of writing' in this 'of whatever kind' sense.

That this structure is most perspicuous in what we already call 'writing' provides a strategic reason for its generalization. But taking and retaining that old name also ensures an effective intervention into the fabric and the evaluative order of the philosophical heritage that has hitherto dominated the subject. As we have seen, the fundamental motif of that fabric is that it relegates writing to a position of debased secondariness: the graphic signifier of the phonetic signifier of signified senses or ideal thought-contents or meanings (the presence of an 'order of pure intelligibility', or *logos*). If, however, anything that could function as a means of communication must possess, in its iterability, the structure of writing, the traditional conception of the sign must give way to an understanding of generalized 'writing', a conception of marks that are, in their essential iterability, *irreducible to anything that can be simply present in the present*. The metaphysical tradition that conceives the being of every being in terms of presence or persisting presence, and which conceives meaning in terms of an order of pure intelligibility or pure ideal *logos* potentially present to the mind or spirit or intelligence of Man, finds itself *dismantled by resources internal to its own construction*. Hence, and here we finally see the work of the word that has become so closely associated with Derrida's text, *the form of argument is a de-construction*, not the proposal of a new or rival construction.

In this chapter and the preceding one, I have followed the attempt in Derrida's text to call into question the very idea of the linguistic sign as something to be construed in terms of the unity of or relation between an outer or in any case *sensible* representation or expression ('signifier') and an inner or in any case *ideal* thought-content or meaning ('signified'). Working within the conceptuality of the tradition, we are brought to see a profoundly therapeutic point to affirming, against the dominant *logos*-centred construction of the tradition, what we might call the first consequence of the short argument for retaining the word 'writing' (stated at the end of the last chapter): that *anything that accompanied writing* (anything that would seem to give these supposedly 'dead' marks 'life') *would just be more writing*. There is in this criticism of the classic conception, in a formulation I will have to clarify in a moment, a 'reduction *of* meaning – that is, of the signified'.

While this formulation risks misunderstanding, it puts Derrida's argument into a relation to the philosophical tradition that is fundamental to it. For in so far as philosophy has involved a commitment to achieving what we might call a 'reduction *to* meaning' (as we saw at the start of the last chapter), then Derrida's rehabilitation of writing will necessarily take the form of a radical critique of traditional philosophy.

However, as I say, Derrida's contrasting effort at a 'reduction *of* meaning' could easily be misunderstood. Indeed, it invites – and has invited – the idea that Derrida's de-constructive thought (presumably incoherently) proposes the *elimination* of the very idea of 'meaning'. And there are remarks which would seem to support an eliminativist reading of Derrida on meaning. For example, he (presumably incoherently) writes that 'writing literally means nothing'. Remarks like this make it seem that Derrida wants to make theoretical claims that would conflict with a life with language that is (I would think) irreducibly committed to talk of meaning. However, as should now be clear, the conception of writing outlined by the argument from iterability does not aim to eliminate ordinary (and hence iterable) talk of meaning and understanding but to criticize the classical conception of meaning – where the only meaning that *is* one would be a meaning that is *one* – embedded in the idea of an event of human speech that would express an ideally pure presence, a pure ideality that would be fully present in the present. Indeed, as Derrida immediately goes on to insist in the passage from his essay 'The Ends of Man' that affirms the 'reduction *of* meaning', this is *not* a matter of 'erasing or destroying meaning', but 'a question of determining the possibility of meaning on the basis of a "formal" organisation which in itself has no meaning'. This '"formal" organisation' is, we now see, the system of general writing, or as he puts it in the passage from *Of Grammatology* with which we began Chapter 4, 'a determined textual system', which is the very element of our being, the 'form' of our life (and not only human life). Purity, on the other hand, the ideal purity of a pure ideality, the classic idea of 'meaning', is never to be had in the present event of such writing. The irreducible singularity of every such event, the specific 'here and now' of marks put into play, could not emerge as such (as a singular event of writing) unless 'the eventhood' of this event was 'in itself . . . repetitive or citational in its structure, or rather, since those two words may lead to confusion: iterable'. Geoffrey Bennington frames the nerve of Derrida's response to a tradition tainted by the tantalization of purity in the following formulation:

> What might look like a negative contingency which might affect or compromise the ideal purity of an event is integrated into the description of that event as a condition of possibility which is simultaneously the condition of the *a priori* impossibility of the event's ever achieving that ideal purity.

As Derrida puts it elsewhere, 'contrary to what our desire cannot fail to be tempted into believing', the philosophical ideal of present meaning, *the* matter for thinking in traditional philosophy, *the* 'thing itself' that philosophy thinks it should 'get back to', 'always steals away'.

One of the myths around Derrida I have been trying to dispel in this book is that he is a kind of sceptic or nihilist who doubts or denies that we ever mean anything or affirms that our words mean nothing. We have now been round the houses on the fault within Derrida text that gives rise to that myth. Should we say that because Derrida proposes the view that because every element of signification has an iterable or *différantial* identity, he is committed to the idea that nothing in fact ever really means anything? Not at all. It is not a suggestion that we never really manage to say anything or are condemned to fall short of ever really meaning anything. Nevertheless, his arguments around iterability and *différance* should make enigmatic the idea of meaning something by what we still call 'signs'.

Indeed, the whole point of his *manner of speaking* of iterability and *différance* derives from what Derrida regards as the philosophical heritage that 'we are already in the midst of' and which we cannot simply reject or overcome; namely, the one that conceives of every signifier as something which 'is put in place of the thing itself, the present thing' (whether that 'thing' is construed as a real or an ideal presence). When we do not have the thing itself present, we say, we can speak about it; 'we go through the detour of signs'. This *philosophical commonplace* belongs to the picture of human language that Derrida interrogates. His questions are not directed at high-level theories of meaning but the 'structure of signs as classically determined'. On this very general picture, 'the sign is conceivable only on the *basis* of the presence that it defers and *moving toward* the deferred presence that it aims to reappropriate'. Derrida's counter-conception is not to think that the commonplace has it almost right, only the final restoration of presence never arrives, but that the picture of the sign as deferred presence keeps in view a misleading picture of a final moment of restored presence. The Derridean manner of speaking that thinks through *différance* is intended as a corrective to that misleading picture that 'here is criticized and displaced'; a corrective to the idea that the ordinary functioning of language is based on or aims at presence or the representation of presence.

Starting where we are, with a picture of signs as deferred presence, Derrida attempts to find elements of our thought that can be turned against the dominant picture, and thus help to depose 'the privilege [that is] the ether of metaphysics': 'the privilege granted to presence'. As Derrida accepts, a de-constructive thought that has its ground in an effort to call into question 'the metaphysics of presence' is 'of the Heideggerian type'. In fact, Derrida's conception of the 'text' (which is not, as we have already noted, restricted exclusively to *human* marks and traces) is not simply Heidegger's 'world' (which is thus restricted). Nevertheless, it may have been noticed already by some readers that Derrida's text is, in many ways, strikingly Heideggerian. That's right, they are always close. However, they are not the same. This will come out in a particularly striking way in Chapter 8 when the idea of the human difference to other animals is directly examined.

Chapter 7
Politics and justice

In the early 1990s, there took place what has been called a 'turn in Derrida's thinking': an ethical and political turn. With the publication of his essay 'Force of Law: The "Mystical Foundation of Authority"' in 1992, it became impossible not to register an effort on Derrida's part to identify connections between his 'philosophico-deconstructive questioning' and wider social and political concerns. Deconstruction, the movement of the dismantling of the Western philosophical heritage (which was disclosed as 'ethnocentric' and hence already never simply philosophical through and through), was not to be thought of merely as a procedure or practice or process that promised a more just theoretical end or some kind of judicious advance for critical thinking, but as the very movement of justice in its relation to law: 'Deconstruction', Derrida announced, 'is justice'.

Many readers saw the prospect of something really salutary arriving here. With the essay 'Force of Law', Derrida's text became 'politicized', his work seemed finally to get political, with deconstruction expressed in 'newly politicized language'. With this new turn in his thinking, the Derridean text might now be put to work to help promote 'a rendering of justice' which would enable us to pass beyond 'a sense of disjuncture, of time out of joint'. Derrida suddenly appeared as someone who could put the world, the time, to rights, setting this as the task for the intellectual. A new Mr Fixit, a new Marx even.

As we shall see in this chapter, there certainly is something like an ethical and political turn in Derrida's thinking from the 1990s on. However, the vision of the arrival of a thinker who might assist us in learning finally how to live and finally putting the world to rights, is, thankfully, quite mistaken. In this chapter, I will first try to get things straight with regard to the significance of a turning point in the path of Derrida's work, and then explore what I take to be the most original and thought-provoking ideas that are worked on beyond it.

From the margin to the centre

I want to take a run-up to the turning point by considering the way in which the system of interpretation of writing that has dominated in the age of the sign is disrupted by Derrida's deconstructive argumentation. In a rare methodological clarification, he describes it as an 'intervention' that effects 'a reversal . . . and a general displacement' of the traditional evaluative hierarchy which privileges speech over writing. However, in a gesture which is fundamental to Derrida's conception of inscription as always already situated inhabitation, we can now see that this deconstruction of the traditional construction does not 'destroy structures from the outside', on the contrary it is 'not possible and effective . . . except by inhabiting those structures' in a novel way. Indeed, as we have seen, Derrida's discussion works over that structure (shakes it up) by taking an acknowledged but *marginalized* concept ('writing') from within it and putting that to work against the evaluative order that dominates it. So this deconstructive reading is not an effort at 'destroying the tradition', but rather an affirmation of what in the heritage 'has always resisted the prior organization of forces . . . the dominant force organizing the hierarchy that we may refer to, in brief, as logocentric'. Thus, in Derrida's text, a graphematic turn makes known as such a movement of logocentric construction which, in fact and in principle, has always also been a movement undergoing graphematic deconstruction. In his affirmation of what resists the logocentric construction, Derrida's text forges a future for the heritage from within it that also takes it beyond its dominant trajectory.

Although the deconstruction of logocentric structures is characterized by reversal *and* displacement of the old evaluative hierarchy of speech and writing (it is not 'writing' in the usual sense that performs the deconstructive shake-up), it is important to see that, in terms of its modal logic (in terms, that is, of the logic of possibilities) the basic pattern of Derrida's argument against the tradition is one of reversal. For example, for the logocentric tradition, the only possible concept (a concept that really *is* one) is a concept that is *one*, and hence (in the terms of the dominant heritage) a supposed 'concept' marked by *irreducible* polysemia is impossible, unthinkable, strictly nonsensical. In his modal reversal, Derrida will affirm instead that the only possible concept – the only concept worthy of the name – is (in the terms of the heritage) the impossible concept. Hence the formulation invoked by Geoffrey Bennington cited towards the end of the last chapter where we come to see that the condition of possibility of a text-event is the condition of impossibility of it attaining the 'ideal purity' required by the classic conception of sense.

Now, this pattern of argumentative reversal marks a fundamental continuity in Derrida's text, both in his early deconstruction of the metaphysics of presence, and in the later more explicitly ethical and political writings. As Bennington was in fact the first to see, the movement from 'early' to 'later' Derrida is best regarded merely as *a shift of emphasis* from a focus on traditionally marginalized predicates to a focus on rather more traditionally central ones. But nothing changes here in method or approach. Indeed, I want to suggest that Derrida's work after his writings on writing, *différance*, and iterability continued to think how 'the only possible *x*' should occur 'under the form of the impossible'. Derrida summarizes the logic of his later analyses of concepts central to our understanding of the ethical significance of our relations to others as follows:

> For instance, that the only possible hospitality is impossible hospitality . . . I would say exactly the same for the gift. I would say exactly the same for forgiveness. So I am trying to elaborate a logic, and I would call this a 'logic', in which the only possible x (and I mean here any rigorous concept of x) is 'the impossible x', and to do so without being caught in an absurd, nonsensical discourse.

The point of the modal reversal of tradition is to suggest that the range of cases positioned by the tradition as possible (or as 'the possibilities of the phenomena') does not do justice to what is really 'worthy of the name' in the phenomenon in question. A real or true possibility, by contrast (one really worthy of the name), will be one that breaks beyond the order of the merely possible (as the tradition has it), and is to that extent impossible. So the only (really and truly) possible is (in the terms of the classical heritage) the impossible.

For example, consider the traditional logic of the ethics of forgiveness. It would insist that the only possible forgiveness (the only forgiveness worthy of the name) is a forgiveness that forgives the forgivable (anything else is nonsense). And then the logic of the modal reversal would be that the only possible forgiveness is the impossible forgiveness, and hence an affirmation of an ethical demand to forgive the unforgivable. The only possible forgiveness – the only forgiveness really worthy of the name – is (in the terms of the traditional logic) the impossible forgiveness.

Consider now the 'Aristotelian ideal' of definite sense that, as we have seen, Derrida identifies with philosophy as such. This states that the only possible concept (a concept that really *is* one) is a concept that is *one* (anything else is nonsense). And then the logic of the modal reversal would be that the only possible concept is the impossible concept, and hence an affirmation of a theoretical demand to acknowledge *irreducible* polysemia. The only possible concept – the only concept really worthy of the name – is (in the terms of the traditional logic) the impossible concept.

Finally, consider the ideal that we might identify with traditional political philosophy. This would insist that the only possible community (a community that really *is* one) is a community that is *one*. Well, as we shall see in this chapter, the logic of the modal reversal here would be that the only possible community is the impossible community, and hence an affirmation of a political call for 'a community of singularities' without anything common, a 'community without community'. The only possible community – the only community really worthy of the name – is (in the terms of the traditional logic) the impossible community.

So the idea that we need to distinguish an 'early' and 'later' Derrida, as is sometimes suggested, should not be taken to imply a change of view, still less change in the logic of his claims. Again, there is no significant change of approach or method but simply a change of emphasis: from forays into the margins of philosophy towards (and with those forays in hand) forays into concepts at the centre of our ethical and political concerns. To suppose that the earlier work simply lacked such ethical and political concerns would therefore be doubly misleading. Not only would it be naive to think that a text that opens – opens in its opening sentence – by announcing that it constitutes an effort to 'focus on the *ethnocentrism* which, everywhere and always, had controlled the concept of writing' was not already deeply ethical and political, but it would fail to see that the affirmation of the impossible entailed by writing a preface to what remains to come was already a profoundly ethical and political gesture.

Nevertheless, it is true to say that the ethico-political orientation of deconstruction, what one might call a concern precisely for *ethical politics*, came to the fore in a more direct and less elliptical manner in Derrida's later writings – in his writings, adverted to above, on hospitality, on the gift, on forgiveness, and then, in the wake of the event named 'the-end-of-communism' or 'the-fall-of-the-Berlin-wall', two books (*Specters of Marx* and *Politics of Friendship*) on political community.

Derrida's confidence in this new work was sometimes less assured than one had come to expect. In the books on political community, for example, he talks of the 'inchoate form' of his remarks, and confesses the limits of his 'competence to speak on these themes'. Nevertheless, as always, he was still determined to pursue this work in a deconstructive manner: his thought was still 'inscribed, undertaken, and understood in the very element of the language it calls into question, struggling at the heart of [political concepts] that are themselves in the grips of auto-deconstructive movement'. And the concepts he explores here are not just any political concepts either. They are the very ones which are at the heart of the understanding of politics and political community that belongs to European societies in their paradigm form in the modern nation state: concepts of fraternity, equality, friendship, and the ties of these to blood and soil.

So the writings of the turn started to explore concepts at the heart of classical political theory. That did not mean, however, that Derrida's text became an undertaking in 'political theory'. In a lecture given at the University of Sussex almost exactly 30 years after the publication of *Of Grammatology*, 30 years after his first effort to take steps 'beyond the closure of knowledge', and to write in the form of an impossible preface, Derrida speaking in his good but imperfect English put it, rather perfectly nonetheless, like this:

> I'm not proposing a . . . political theory because what I'm saying, exceeds, precisely, knowledge. In its extreme and more essential form it has to do with something which cannot become a theoreme, it is something which simply has to be known, there is some type of experience, of political experience . . . which cannot be simply

> the object of a theory. Which is not an anti-theoretical move; I think political theory is necessary, but I try to articulate this necessity of a political theory with something in politics . . . which cannot, for structural reasons, become the object of knowledge, of a theory, of a theoreme. So, it's not a political theory . . . and it's not a deconstructive politics either. I don't think that there is such a thing as a deconstructive politics, if by the name 'politics' we mean a programme, an agenda, or even the name of a regime . . . . So, I don't think that what I'm engaged in . . . can be called political theory or deconstructive politics, but I think that given . . . the premises of what I have been doing before these last books, the time has come for me to say something more about politics. Not simply a political theory, a deconstructive politics, but to say something about politics is again not simply a speculative gesture: it's a concrete and personal commitment, and this performative commitment is part of what I'm writing. *Specters of Marx*, before being a text about Marx's theory, Marx's heritage, is, let's say, a personal commitment at a certain moment, in a certain form, in a singular fashion.

Let us follow the path of this 'personal commitment'.

Political community in deconstruction

I think a number of readers of Derrida's text would have been surprised by the personal commitments that emerged in the book *Specters of Marx*. In particular, like Marx – but explicitly *without* Marx – Derrida affirmed again and again 'I am not a Marxist', and he re-iterated that he was not among those in his post-war generation of French intellectuals who hid from the 'totalitarian terror' that had overtaken Eastern Europe and the 'socio-economic disasters of Soviet bureaucracy'. He was, he says, always opposed to *de facto* 'Marxism' or 'communism'. So he was not at all sorry, in this sense, to see the 'end of communism'. However, though not on the extreme left of Marxists or post-Marxist leftists, Derrida insisted that he did not oppose Marxism or communism out of conservative or reactionary motivations, and he wasn't writing in the early 1990s to join those who were proclaiming the coming of or arrival of an 'end of history' and who 'find the means to puff out their chests with the good conscience of capitalism, liberalism and the virtues of *present*, which is to say in fact, *past* forms of the electoral and parliamentary apparatus'. Things are not so rosy. Derrida highlighted a number of massive counter-evidences to the end of history idea, but in the next few pages I want to pick up on his response to just two distinctive features of our time, features that could concern anyone concerned with the future of democracy.

The first feature is bound up with the fact that the present forms of parliamentary democracy are actually past forms. The European model of parliamentary democracy in the nation state emerged hand in hand with a certain level of development of communication technologies. However, the former has not undergone anything like the kind of transformative mutation we have witnessed and are still witnessing in the latter. This is a fact – and it is a problem. Derrida's worry is that these changes do not leave the old model unaffected. Indeed, according to Derrida, the forms of parliamentary representativity which emerged within the space and time of a certain level of technological development have been 'dangerously weakened' by the 'techno-tele-media apparatuses and by new rhythms of information and communication' that are developing at speed and at speeds which radically transform (and do not just extend) the distances and times of the world, changes which are transforming the world and disrupt the very idea of a localizable 'place' of the 'public space' that had belonged to the old nation states of Europe.

'If there is a tendency not to respect professional politicians' in our time, Derrida suggests, this may not be a personal fault of politicians. They may well be decent people who are genuinely striving to think well about political and social conditions. But what can they do? More and more, or even solely, they become 'characters in the media's representation', in a global 24-hour media which has fundamentally transformed the public space in which their 'legitimate power' in nation states had previously been embedded. In our time, Derrida regretfully notes, 'actors in politics often risk being no more than TV actors'.

So Derrida did not join a media frenzy which celebrated the end of communism, or euphoric proclamations that heralded the 'good news' that the globalization of 'liberal democracy and the market economy' will mark the end of history. 'Deconstruction has never been Marxist', but nor is it simply 'anti-Marxist' either. Indeed, he suggests that his early work on the deconstruction of logocentrism 'would have been impossible and un-thinkable in a pre-Marxist space'. However, the Marx that had been taken over by orthodoxy was not anything that Derrida wanted to associate himself with in the 1960s – nor 30 years later. Nevertheless, a certain 'spirit of Marxism' should, he thinks, be affirmed. And he wagers that he will not be alone in thinking that. In an effort to form or forge a kind of 'holding together' of friends who are scattered all over the world, and who may not even know each other, 'the disparate itself', Derrida sought a new alliance 'without organization, without party, without nation, without State, without property', an alliance that he called a 'new International'.

To understand this gesture, we first need to be clear that Derrida is not against any of the things he lists here (political organization, political parties, the nation, state, property), as if they are the *a priori* objectionables of some normative political theory. However, he is trying to understand what today goes beyond them, and to think, in this time of 'a phase of decisive mutation', the possibility of a certain 'democracy to come' that will no longer be limited by present, that is to say, by past forms of political democracy and representativity, and which would be better adjusted, or less problematically dis-adjusted to 'the rhythms of information and communication' that are transforming our world and the spaces of politics.

Making its way within the space we already inhabit, Derrida's text strives to retrieve a dimension of the political heritage which already de-limits it, de-territorializes it, which already takes it beyond its present nation state limit. And he finds it in the fundamentally democratic but 'abstract and potentially indifferent thought' of 'number and equality'. This principle *can* be allied to – and *has* traditionally been allied to – a territorializing risk that Derrida calls 'terrifying': namely, an idea of 'homogenizing calculability' that confidently knows how to count some people 'in' and some people 'out' of the democratic order; the classic idea of the rootedness of those who count 'in' in 'land and blood'. According to this old idea, *we are the same*, you and I and every other who counts. 'We' are not the other, and you and I and every other that counts count as 'the same', share a fundamental equality, because we *naturally* belong together – we are brothers, friends, we have roots, natural roots, in a given territory. This is a dimension of traditional forms of democratic community from which Derrida's text wants to save nothing. However, and at least for now, the name democracy *also* carries within it something else entirely:

> the power of universalizing beyond the State and the nation, the account taken of anonymous and irreducible singularities, infinitely different and thereby indifferent to particular difference, to the raging quest for identity corrupting the most indestructible desires of the idiom.

While democracy is a political form that has been caught up in desires for equality based on supposedly natural ties of blood and soil, Derrida retrieves within that desire a quasi-cosmopolitan love that cherishes and cultivates the singularity of every other, and which powerfully resists ethnic or national homogeneity and identitarian emotions.

This quasi-cosmopolitan indifference to particular difference that cherishes the idiomatic and the singular highlights a second feature of our time that should concern us today – a concern with justice. The 'new International' is not a new 'international of communist parties', it does not attempt to institute communism as a regime; indeed, it does not even appeal to some kind of 'common' – a class commonality or ethnic or national or even international community. Nevertheless, it belongs to this worldwide alliance of scattered friends to bear a particular concern with the fact that international law today is dominated by particular nation states and their techno-economic military power. This is not a fault in the law as such. And Derrida does not hesitate to pay tribute to and to salute those who work in international institutions and attempt to free them from such domination. But this domination is a fact – and it is a problem. The worry Derrida raises on this topic belongs to a line of thought that goes right back to Plato:

> Plato excludes the possibility of realizing an ideal state as long as philosophers do not reign over it, as long as the kings and sovereigns, the 'dynasts' who dispose of power are not philosophers – that is as long as *philosophia* is not bound to political power: in other words as long as justice (which must be distinguished from law) is not bound to power, as long as justice is not one with force.

The 'new International' is, in a certain way, a new figure – a newly democratized figure – of the philosopher king. It belongs to the movement (carried, it must be said, in waves of laughter over the centuries, but philosophers know they have to take their time) which would want to see '*philosophia* bound to political power', a world in which justice is bound to power.

Who, then, is part of this movement without party, without organization, without membership cards, of this new International? First of all, like philosophy itself, it is open to all, no one is excluded: 'barely deserving the name community, the new International belongs only to anonymity'. However, the responsibility that falls on those who belong to this scattered community without community, though it falls in principle on anyone and does not exclude anyone, does not, *today*, fall on everyone *indifferently*. On the contrary, Derrida insists that it falls *today* to some 'more imperatively' or 'by priority' or more 'urgently' than it does to others. Derrida identifies who it particularly singles out as follows. They are:

- those who will have already managed to resist 'a certain hegemony of the Marxist dogma';
- those who have insisted on conceiving and on practising this resistance 'without showing any leniency towards reactionary, conservative or neoconservative, anti-scientific or obscurantist temptations';
- 'those who have ceaselessly proceeded in, I will dare to say, in a deconstructive fashion, in the name of a new Enlightenment for the century to come'.

In short, this fundamentally anonymous, radically universalizable responsibility is not 'just anyone's' at all. The only thing one can be sure of here is: it is Derrida's – and those who are his ilk.

We live in a time of dis-location, of de-localization – of 'lovers, families, nations'. How are we to conceive of a politics beyond the politics of the 'community of friends' that has dominated modern Europe and the West for over two hundred years? As we have seen, the canonical politics of democratic friendship loves, cherishes, and cultivates equality among brothers: calculability, countability, where you count units, voters, citizens, voices, indifferently, equally. ('Democracy means, minimally, equality.') The question is, however, whether it is possible to think a politics of democratic friendship that could free itself from the terrifying threat of homogenization, the ethno-nationalist politics of identity, which has so profoundly marked its passage into our time.

As we are beginning to see, such a possibility can be retrieved in the democratic idea that each one (everyone, anyone) counts as one. To affirm that each counts as one can mean that each shares *the same* identity. This is to abstract entirely from particular differences between ordinary singularities. And yet the experience of the radical unreplaceability, the absolute unsubstitutability, the fundamental uniqueness of the singular other, belongs just as much to friendship – especially in the concrete encounter with the friend one loves – as does equality and reciprocity. The question is, then, whether there could be a politics of democratic friendship that would cherish *both* the equality of everyone *and* 'take into account and respect the heterogeneous singularity of everyone'. This would be a politics that would thereby resist best 'the raging quest for homogeneity and identity' that dominates the canonical concept of friendship and which has dominated the politics of democracy for so long (the equality of brothers, the community of brother-friends with roots in a territory, blood and soil and so on, as the natural foundation of the nation). Is it possible to think of 'a democracy beyond the limits of the classical political model' that would allow us to 'think differently this double injunction of equality for everyone and respect for singularity'?

The centuries of Greco-Christianity, the inscription of place which has called itself (to be) 'Europe', has freed a de-localizing movement of democratic political desire. But where is it heading? Let us track it.

Democratic desire

Derrida specifies the basic characteristics of a democratic political desire in terms of the 'double injunction' identified at the heart of the politics of friendship, now figured as necessary (but not sufficient) conditions for democracy:

> There is no democracy without respect for irreducible singularity or alterity, but there is no democracy with the 'community of friends' (*koína ta philōn*), without the calculation of majorities, without identifiable, stabilizable, representable subjects, all equal. The two laws are irreducible one to the other. Tragically irreconcilable and forever wounding. The wound itself opens with the necessity of having to count one's friends, to count the others, in the economy

> of one's own, there where every other is altogether other. But where every other is *equally* altogether other. More serious than a contradiction, political desire is forever borne by the disjunction of these two laws. It also bears the chance and the future of a democracy whose ruin it constantly threatens but whose life, however, it sustains, like life itself, at the heart of its *divided virtue*, the inadequacy to itself.

On this account, the political desire for democracy is forever destined to its own non-satisfaction: it is a preference for what can never be realized in a final form of ideal adequacy. Its 'divided virtue' entails that a certain 'inadequacy to itself' (the condition of being insufficiently democratic) is irreducible. Any putative democratic institution, for example a democratic state, immediately and interminably falls short with respect to what is desired. But falling short here is not failing to realize an ideal adequacy that one day, in the future (even an ideal future), might be made present. With democracy, perhaps uniquely, there can be no orientation or directedness towards such an ideal end. Instead, from case to case, one can only strive to *endure* the open wound, committing oneself *in the name of democracy* to the necessity of undertaking deliberations and decisions which must, at once and without delay, betray the 'community of friends', by having to calculate (or count as the same) with the incalculable (with the uncountable – since each one is the only one).

Democracy on this understanding is the name for what is aimed at by a political desire – which is obviously not alien to a religious desire – to cherish and to cultivate the irreducible *singularity* of every other (and which, for that reason, most strongly resists the politics of homogeneity and identity that so clearly marked old Europe, and which has not gone away). But, for the same reason, it is also a political desire to cherish and to cultivate *equality*. For the friend of democratic desire, there is no question of demanding the other to be just like me, to share my identity as something to have 'in common' with me. Democratic desire aims at the realization of a 'community of friends' that would be an alliance of singularities who are infinitely other, each one the only one. (The realization of a new International indeed.) But that is why it also aims at the realization of a 'community of friends' in which each one can be recognized as, in that respect, just like the other, each one fundamentally equal to every other. At every step, the *aporia* (the experience of being without a way out, without a path, *a-poros*) endures. It is the politics of democratic politics without a final end.

It is for this reason that democracy represents the 'other' of every politics that would be elaborated in terms of a determinate teleo-messianic conception of *the proper end of Man*; it is the other of every politics with a redemptive end in sight. As a political desire, the commitment to democracy desires what is neither given in the present nor even given in the anticipation of an ideal future present, and hence it is the desire for something of which there is, as Levinas puts it, 'no adequate idea'. At issue, then, is an orientation in the world by a political desire that is constitutionally aporetic. Fundamentally akin to the provisional condition of finding within the old language *a new manner of speaking*, efforts faithfully to think and act in the name of democracy make moves within the 'economy of one's own' – an economy stabilized in a language or a culture or a heritage – that are experienced as striving towards a 'we don't know what' that lies ahead of us. A future in relation to which our today is experienced as a preface for what remains to come, for what is not yet written, beyond anticipation, beyond knowledge.

Taking us back, as they do, to the opening chapters of this book, these ideas link up the challenge to re-think politics beyond the politics of the end of Man with the mutation within the Western heritage that Derrida had highlighted from his earliest writings. The philosopher David Wiggins, writing explicitly in 'a time after Darwin', but which is also and equally clearly a time after Copernicus, offers something of a summary of this mutation in the following passage:

> Unless we are Marxists, we are more resistant [today] than the eighteenth- or nineteenth-centuries knew how to be [to] attempts to locate the meaning of human life or human history in mystical or metaphysical conceptions – in the emancipation of mankind, or progress, or the onward advance of Absolute Spirit. It is not that we have lost interest in emancipation or progress themselves. But whether temporarily or permanently, we have more or less abandoned the idea that the importance of emancipation or progress (or a correct conception of spiritual advance) is that these are marks by which our minute speck in the universe can distinguish itself as the spiritual focus of the cosmos.

Before tracing this de-centring movement into our time more closely with Derrida, I want to broach a worry that might be felt with Wiggins' rather rapid dismissal of Marxism. The worry is that unless we *are* Marxists – or at least unless we can still frame an objective conception of what is proper to the good life for Man, *the proper end of Man* – we have no basis on which to assess whether we are moving towards or away from the attainment of a better form of life *at all*. Hence any continued interest in 'the importance of emancipation and progress' would seem to be meaningless. Wiggins claims that our increased resistance to historico-messianic narratives does *not* imply that we have lost interest in 'emancipation or progress themselves'. But can we, today, retain that interest – and not be Marxist?

This question invites us to acknowledge that *we* belong to societies with a history whose self-understanding simply cannot be radically dissociated from a Marxist heritage. As Derrida notes, 'whether they wish it or know it or not, all men and women, all over the earth, are today, to a certain extent, the heirs of Marx and Marxism'. There is a complication to every discourse that would say that our interest in emancipation or progress could be radically non-Marxist or can simply do without Marx. Especially if we think we are not Marxist. Here is Derrida again:

> A messianic promise, even if it was not fulfilled, at least in the form in which it was uttered, even if it rushed headlong toward an ontological content, will have imprinted an inaugural and unique mark in history. And whether we like it or not, whatever consciousness we have of it, we cannot not be its heirs.

Unless we are going to be naively unwitting Marxists, we had better attend to this inheritance. We need to attend to the spectres of Marx and Marxism. Especially today, when it is so often announced, naively, that Marxism is dead.

I will come back to this, but first we need to acknowledge that Wiggins' political naivety is coupled with an important historical insight. It is, I think, plainly true that

> we are more resistant [today] than the eighteenth- or nineteenth-centuries knew how to be [to] attempts to locate the meaning of human life or human history in mystical or metaphysical conceptions – in the emancipation of mankind, or progress, or the onward advance of Absolute Spirit.

It is as one of the last great attempts to elaborate a grand historico-messianic narrative of the emancipation and progress of Man that Marxism has its place in Wiggins' account.

If I was a Marxist, or a Marxist through and through, I would have an understanding of the significance of our lives which showed our present condition as alienated and which pointed towards a historical movement of de-alienation, a historical movement in which it will all come right in the end, if we can only get our collective act together and build that revolution. Is Wiggins taking unjustified advantage of the 'we' when he implies that, at least for most of us these days, *we don't believe that*, we can't fall back on a philosophy of the history of the alienation and de-alienation of Man like that? I don't think he is. In our time, we need to shift decisively from thinking in (classical messianic) terms of an end of Man in which we *finally learn how to live* to (but holding on to something of that messianism) learning to endure interminably learning how to live, learning to live without the promise of *finally* learning how to live. For Derrida, this shift is totally inseparable from the graphematic mutation which outlined the closure of the logocentric age of the sign, an age dominated by an ethnocentric vision of human history as the teleological movement towards the end of Man, and hence is totally inseparable from the liberation in our world of a strictly interminable desire for 'democracy to come'.

Historical theodicies, histories of the world with a redemptive end, whether theist or atheist, can only regard the not-so-teleological relation to the future affirmed by Derrida's text as a counsel of despair or at best an excuse for quietist inaction. However, from the inside of democratic desire, the only future for ourselves (for our language, our culture, our heritage) worth having is a future that is experienced as yet to come. It is a hope for freedom and progress that – for both believers and non-believers alike – can get along without the idea of what Hegel called 'the attainability of a definite result' in an end of history in which Man would have finally achieved a supposedly ideal form of human community, a community in which he could become actually what he always had been potentially, radically de-alienated, free and equal: a community that, finally, really *is* one because it is a human community which, finally, is *one*.

Some may feel that without the good news of such a mirage in the desert, without faith in the advent of a redemptive end of Man in an ideal community, we are left standing still, left 'at the starting line'. But, as Derrida affirms, it may also give one the 'strength and speed', here and now, to act: to do everything one can to keep the space open for unknown friends of democratic desire to come.

So, in Derrida's text, we find that it is the '*hope, beyond all "messianisms", of a universalizable culture of singularities*' that occupies the space reserved for the classic interest in emancipation and progress that belonged to the time before our today. It takes place, here and now, wherever we affirm the logic of the modal reversal outlined at the start of this chapter: that the only possible community is the impossible community. And so, within the limits in which any such judgement is possible, the lives that are of most interest in our time will belong to those participants for whom *the idea of finally having done with the question of how to live* – let's call these participants 'philosophers', whoever they are – is experienced most intensely or most keenly as something, today, *to resist*.

To resist what, then? First and foremost, the rule of every *doxa* of messianic arrival. On the other hand, the punch about resistance just delivered has other aims too, including the one I have already identified, with Wiggins, as the last great effort at a classical historico-messianic vision of emancipation and progress towards a fully human community: a conception claiming to possess the *truth of Man* and which thus promises that we *can* learn, *finally*, how to live in a proper *end of Man*. I mean Marxism.

Given the increasingly secularized way in which the world and the significance of our lives have been grasped and lived in the last three hundred years or so, it is, perhaps, not surprising that Marxism, uniquely, has been able to survive the increased resistance to historico-messianic narratives that marks our time. That it should *not* continue do so in its classic form is, in my view, the central lesson of Derrida's brilliant but difficult text *Specters of Marx*. Like Wiggins, Derrida wants to preserve in our time – and in his case, to preserve, without naivety, from Marxism – something of the classic interest in emancipation and progress. However, Derrida, again like Wiggins, wants to inherit that anew and *non-classically*, that is *without* the idea of a final end of Man and everything associated with it. Indeed, what he says he does *not* want to inherit from Marxism is: *'almost everything'*.

On the other hand, and without ever capitulating to Marxist intimidation, what Derrida's text wants to keep alive and inherit from Marxism – and against the 'religion of capital' that confronts us on all sides today – is its emancipatory spirit. Derrida's work, especially his later work, explicitly called for a form of thinking and questioning that could do more than merely occupy itself with concerns inside the 'monastic ivory tower' of professional academia. Philosophico-deconstructive questioning should be concerned to change things, and to 'change things . . . not only in the profession but . . . in the world'. Indeed, what, in the essay 'Force of Law', he calls 'the experience of inadequation' of existing laws with respect to justice is fundamental to his effort consistently to follow, as far as possible – though insisting as well that it is not 'a true distinction' – the early modern philosopher Montaigne's contrast between laws (*droit*) and justice. And Derrida is equally insistent that the *aporias* he attends to should in no way stop one in one's tracks, and thus prevent one from getting actively involved in 'juridico-political battles'. On the contrary, what is required, he argues, is precisely not to take 'emancipatory battles' beyond the law, but to take the law, or at least 'the element of calculation' that he regards as essential to legal reasoning, into every field in which there is an appeal to justice.

The idea of the calculability of law here relates to the generality of a rule, and of reasoning that in principle would apply to anyone. The corresponding 'incalculability' of justice that Derrida insists upon relates to decisions which are themselves always singular, concerning individuals or collectivities that are radically irreplaceable in situations that ultimately resist generalization. Law, Derrida argues, is nevertheless the best way, the most *just* way, we have for organizing a response – a politicizing response not in the least excluded – to such singularities: 'incalculable justice *requires* us to calculate', it requires us to do what we can in 'emancipatory battles that remain and will have to remain in progress'. Moreover, it requires us to do what we can, not only in already identified 'territories of juridico-politicization', but also in new and presently still marginal areas. Derrida runs through a list of examples, many of which would be familiar in what is today called applied philosophy:

> the area of laws on the teaching and practice of languages, the legitimization of canons, the military use of scientific research, abortion, euthanasia, problems of organ transplantation, extra-uterine conception, bio-engineering, medical experimentation, the social treatment of AIDS, the macro- or micro-politics of drugs, the homeless, and so on, without forgetting, of course, the treatment of what we call animal life, animality.

It is in view of the deep need to find a just response to emancipatory battles like these that Derrida will insist that 'it is *just* that there be *law*'.

In the next chapter, we will see how Derrida takes on questions concerning the last of his examples here: the deconstructive treatment of the heritage on 'what we call animal life'.

Chapter 8
Man and animal

Deconstructing humanism

In the opening chapter of his great text *Being and Time*, Martin Heidegger broaches an historical interpretation of the way 'we in our time' have become disoriented with regard to an understanding of our own being: 'What stands in the way of the basic question of our being (or leads it off the track) is', he suggests, 'an orientation thoroughly coloured by the anthropology of the ancient [Greek] world [the conception of man as the *zōon logon echon* (*animal rationale*)] and Christianity [the conception of man as made in God's image]'. The understanding of Man, and of what is construed on this understanding as 'proper to Man', that comes down to us from these sources is, as we have already seen, a central theme in Derrida's work. Following Heidegger, he will often refer to it as the classic 'humanist' understanding of Man. Heidegger characterizes humanism as that tradition in which what it calls 'Man' is defined by setting it off as one kind of entity present in the world among other entities (*Homo animalis*). Human beings are not, however, simply equated with mere things in the world or even with other living creatures. On the contrary, humanism accords Man a specific and special difference or dignity denied to all other things: Man is the animal endowed with the capacity for reason or for language; Man is the *ens finitum* [finite being] created by God in God's image.

According to Heidegger, this classic humanist anthropology remains in place in modern philosophy since Descartes: it too conceives human existence primarily in terms of presence and then supplies this animal presence with a unique and distinctive trait. Thus it rejects the fully naturalistic idea that 'the essence of man simply consists in being an animal organism' and proposes that 'this insufficient definition of man's essence [can] be overcome or offset' by adding on to it the idea of man having 'an immortal soul'; or by 'adjoining a mind to the human body' and saying that we are a thinking thing, a self-conscious subject. Thus Heidegger's view is that in post-Cartesian philosophy, where consciousness is the point of departure, humanism remains the background conception: 'In principle we are still thinking of *Homo animalis* – even when . . . this is later posited as subject, person or spirit.'

For Heidegger, then, the two-fold classic humanist anthropology is what 'stands in the way' of achieving an adequate understanding of our being. His own alternative position is (by his own admission) itself an original kind of 'humanism', something evident in his saying that the main problem with classic humanism is not that it set what is distinctively human in the human, Man's '*humanitas*', too high, but rather that it does not set it 'high enough'. It is perhaps on this issue, above all, that Derrida is least faithfully Heideggerian. As we shall see, Derrida does not want to deny the significance we attach to the idea of the difference between human beings and other animals, nor will he give any truck to the fully naturalistic idea that human beings are simply one 'animal organism' among others. On the other hand, according to Derrida, the classic humanist tradition – including Heidegger's original development of that tradition – describes this difference in terms that Derrida finds deeply problematic, both theoretically and, in terms of our treatment of animals today, practically. In this chapter, I want to introduce some of the main lines of Derrida's deconstruction of humanist thinking on this topic.

The principal claim that Derrida makes against the humanist tradition can be summarized with what, in a essay published in

2002 called 'The Animal That Therefore I Am (More to Follow)', he calls his first 'thesis'. While not for a moment questioning our 'common-sense' adherence to the idea of an 'abyssal rupture' between human beings and animals, Derrida's thesis is that this is not to be understood in terms of the picture of 'a unilinear and indivisible line' with 'Man' on one side and the 'Animal' on the other. This thesis will not leave our understanding of what lies on either side of the abyss intact either; neither Man (grasped teleologically in terms of 'the history of the world'), on the one side, nor the homogenizing catch-all category of the 'Animal' or 'Animal Life' (grasped biologistically in terms of the merely or purely natural history of an 'animal organism'), on the other.

The importance of understanding the way Derrida's text calls into question the *logos*-centred idea of Man and the proper end of Man has been stressed throughout this book. As we have seen, from his very earliest writings, Derrida's work of deconstruction was particularly pitted against 'the opposition of nature and culture, animality and humanity, etc.'. However, it was not until he turned towards a more explicit discussion of ethics and politics that the question of animality and the critique of onto-theological humanism really came together.

To help situate Derrida's principal claim against humanism, I want to launch off with a passage from an essay by the philosopher Cora Diamond which highlights a distinction between two ways of thinking about the human/animal difference:

> The difference between human beings and animals is not to be discovered by studies of Washoe or the activities of dolphins. It is not that sort of study or ethology or evolutionary theory that is going to tell us the difference between us and animals: the difference is, I have suggested, a central concept for human life and is more an object of contemplation than observation (though that might be misunderstood; I am not suggesting it is a matter of intuition). One source of confusion here is that we fail to

distinguish between 'the difference between animals and people' and 'the differences between animals and people'; the same sort of confusion occurs in discussions of the relationship of men and women. In both cases people appeal to scientific evidence to show that 'the difference' is not as deep as we think; but all that such evidence can show, or show directly, is that the differences are less sharp than we think. In the case of the difference between animals and people, it is clear that we form the idea of this difference, create the concept of the difference, knowing perfectly well the overwhelmingly obvious similarities.

This comes from one of the best attempts I know to affirm the idea of a difference between human beings and other animals. But proper appreciation of its novelty requires that we situate it within and against the background of standard 'humanistic' attempts to articulate it in the history of philosophy. That history is in fact precisely the one in view in Derrida's elaboration of the logocentric heritage. Indeed, Derrida's text defines logocentrism as 'first of all a thesis regarding the animal, the animal deprived of the *logos*, deprived of the *can-have-the-logos*'. It is the logocentric epoch which has made Diamond's affirmation possible, but it is an epoch dominated by a view of the difference from which it must also be, as far as possible, disentangled.

For reasons I will come back to shortly, while I do not think that the dominant philosophical idea of this difference is simply rooted in 'theoretical' resources, we can still follow Derrida's (Heideggerian) identification of the Greek and Christian sources of the logocentric epoch by taking our theoretical cue from the corresponding Greek and Christian determinations of Man outlined above: the conception of Man as the *zōon logon echon* (*animal rationale*); and the Christian theomorphic idea of Man as made in God's image.

The idea of the difference has been worked on and worked over – made something of – by a heritage that is, I think, fundamentally rooted in these two sources. However, it is clear that this heritage is now losing some of its general appeal. Many today are beginning to think that the idea that the difference is something we humans have *discovered* to be the case ('an object of observation', as Diamond puts it) should *not* be sustained. Derrida, like Diamond, is firmly located among those who are not content with that 'cognitivist' idea of the difference.

However, there is a recoil position taken by some of those who they are among here which is, for Derrida, just as unsatisfactory. The recoil position regards the idea that we have discovered this abyssal difference as a *factual error* on our part, the residue of less enlightened times when we had not got our understanding of nature and ourselves as natural creatures right. Today, some think, we have the power, the theoretical power, to get things right, and regard it as well established that, in fact, we are just another species of living thing, a living thing that ultimately differs from other living things only by degree.

Derrida, like Diamond, completely rejects this recoil position: 'one would have to be more asinine than any beast [*plus bête que les bêtes*]' to believe in 'some homogeneous continuity between what calls itself man and what he calls the animal'. But this does not imply a re-affirmation of classic humanism. On the contrary, in Derrida's text, we find a careful and compelling attempt to negotiate a path between the humanist heritage and asinine biologism. On the one hand, he rejects the classic humanistic assumption that the difference of which it speaks is something we have discovered to be the case (whether through philosophical speculation or through spiritual revelation). On the other hand, however, he rejects the fully naturalistic assumption that our common-sense adherence to the idea of this difference is simply the result of a *defective* means of establishing what is the case, something that has been overcome by today's more powerful scientific understanding of nature and ourselves as natural creatures.

I think Derrida is right to attack both targets. However, in what looks like an either/or situation (the human condition as either, in fact, a radical break from an animal condition or, in fact, in a fundamental continuity with it), his taking on both fronts doesn't seem to leave us with any alternative. Derrida's demand (on the side of a certain naturalism) that we 'take into account a multiplicity of heterogeneous structures and limits' may avoid what he calls a 'crime against animals' (namely corralling them into a single general category of 'the Animal'), but it does nothing to explain the significance we (human beings) attach to the difference 'between what calls *itself* man and what *he* calls the animal'. For example, it does not explain why we do not (except under the most extreme conditions or the most ritualized occasions) eat dead people.

In order to get off the see-saw of classic humanism and modern naturalism, a further step is needed. And this can be achieved once we come to see that the same fundamental *cognitivism* with regard to the significance we attach to the idea of the human/animal difference is at the problematic heart of *both* accounts. Both claim that a proper grasp of its significance is ultimately, *decisively*, a matter of our having adjusted our beliefs to how things really (even essentially) are. This is what we need to resist. That is, to follow Derrida in this area, we need to resist the temptation to affirm in theoretical reflection what David Wiggins has called the appearance of a 'naïve cognitivism' in many people's everyday ethical outlook. Not that a theoretically enlightened thinker – a thinker who is attracted to the idea that the difference between humans and animals is 'more an object of contemplation than observation' – is going to give up on the idea that 'the differences between higher and lower forms of life' are real or is going to suppose that they are simply fictitious. On the contrary, such a thinker can accept that there is an astonishing 'heterogeneous multiplicity of the living' and can comfortably accept that such *differences* are *objective*. However, as Wiggins puts it, this thinker 'will not back down from [the] denial that these differences are *decisive*': 'Such differences', he continues, 'may be important to us. But they depend for their significance upon a framework that is a free construct, not upon something fashioned in a manner that is answerable to how anything really is.' The significance we attach to the *differences*, and in particular the idea we form of the *difference*, is not a matter merely of taking due regard to *objectivity* – or, since what is at issue is the idea of an 'absolute' difference, one can equally well say, not a matter of taking due regard to the *real* structure of subjectivity – as if we had *discovered in the nature of things* an abyssal 'all or nothing' disjunction between, say, rational animality or rational subjectivity, *the truth of Man*, on the one hand, and non-rational animality or non-rational subjectivity (which may be some kind of subjectivity or some kind of proto-subjectivity – or really no kind of subjectivity at all), *the truth of the Animal*, on the other.

It is this anti-cognitivist, historical-constructivist conception that is, I think, the crucial presupposition for dismounting the see-saw between classic humanist discontinuism and modern biologistic continuism. And it is this we find affirmed in Derrida's text.

Beyond the truth of man

The anti-cognitivist claim is that the idea that human life has special significance never was something that, as Wiggins puts it, 'we as a species ever (as we say) found or discovered'. *A fortiori* it is not an error simply to be corrected by a better theory of nature either. Indeed, what is at issue here is the result of processes of a kind that Darwin himself regarded as *contrasting* markedly with the kinds of forces of *natural* selection which are originary in natural history: namely, 'unconstrained inventive processes'. Of course, unlike the splendidly deliberate work of *artificial* selection that fascinated Darwin and which gave rise to numerous new pigeon varieties, the inventive processes which have given rise to the construction upon which depends the significance we attach to the idea of the human difference were, as Wiggins (not unproblematically but bearably) puts it, 'gradual, unconscious and communal'.

Derrida does not doubt that human beings have always identified themselves in ways which include an elaboration of a concept of the human difference, and that this difference is an undeniably central concept in human life. Moreover, he regards it as naive to think that such concepts belong only to an age of pre-scientific myth and superstition. Indeed, as we have seen, the narrative of the progressive movement of the 'becoming-civilized' of Man is also central to the traditional idea of our so-called 'modernity'. And this was never a merely theoretical conception either. Articulating what he calls the founding 'mythography' of Western modernity, it has itself been historically world-forming: informing or imprinting itself on the lives of those who celebrated the unbroken 'golden thread' of (singular) Civilization, and of course, the lives of those who, in the name of that mono-genealogy, lay outside of and did not measure up to what the Europeans of the 19th century called the 'Standard of Civilization'.

Indeed, in Derrida's view the elaboration of this mythography in and as the history of modernity has had fundamental and objective consequences not only for human beings, as a result of the ethnocentric assessment of human differences, but also for animals. There are two sides to this sorry tale. *On the one hand* (the animal hand), and speaking 'from the heart', Derrida claims that 'no one could deny that [an alteration in the human relation to animals] has been accelerating, intensifying, no longer knowing where it is going, for about two centuries, at an incalculable rate and level'; 'no one can deny the *unprecedented* proportions of the subjection [of animals to the well-being of man]', that is taking place in our time. Yet, according to Derrida, we live today mostly in denial, indeed, in a denial of what, in other contexts – in particular, in contexts in which our relation to animals is quite distinctively not to 'animals in general' but an aliveness to *this creature with a life* – their own speaking hearts would find intolerable. So ultimately, despite the alteration in human relations to animals that marks contemporary modernity:

> no one can deny seriously, or deny for very long, that men do all they can in order to dissimulate this cruelty [of the subjection of animals] or to hide it from themselves, in order to organize on a global scale the forgetting or misunderstanding of this violence that some would compare to the worst cases of genocide (there are also animal genocides: the number of species endangered because of man takes one's breath away).

And it is not only a question of driving certain species to extinction either. In 'monstrous' conditions, certain other species are given a 'virtually interminable survival' in the process of their 'industrial . . . production, breeding and slaughter'.

On the other hand (the human hand), this dissimulation and disassociation from what, in the kind of context of human aliveness to animal others just mentioned, no one can deny, is obviously telling of modern humanity too. Talk of an abyssal difference between the human and animal is an expression of the special significance we attach to the idea of the human, and that is no more an error than it is an error to mourn the loss of a friend. But no one can deny, or deny for very long, that this abyssal difference has a crossable frontier. The very concepts through which we express human relationships, concepts that mark a profoundly *non-biological* concept of the human – concepts like friendship or fellowship or companionship – are simply not marked 'for human use only'. On the contrary, the very concepts through which we express this non-biological significance of the human are, as Cora Diamond puts it, distinctively '*labile*'; they are apt to shift, and to shift right across the human/animal boundary. In Derrida's terms, we might say that the *iterability* of these concepts displays what we might call an essential *iteralability*. For example, when one mourns the loss . . . of a friend.

Derrida's recourse to the concept of iterability rather than repeatability in the analysis of writing had already sought to make room for shifts and differences within conceptual identity.

Indeed, that analysis explicitly aimed to capitalize on the (probable) etymological link of *iter*, meaning 'once again', to *itara*, meaning 'other' in Sanskrit, in order to develop a manner of speaking that could capture a link between repetition and alterity, a link between staying the same and being apt to shift. So a certain 'lability' is already at work wherever there is 'writing' in Derrida's refreshed sense. In the kind of case we are concerned with here, however, it is not just a question of a new singular response that retains once again or once more an essentially iterable mark, but the extension of responses characteristic of our responses to human beings *beyond* the human. That we do so respond might suggest that there are occasions when we want to *efface* the idea of the human difference. That is a terribly tempting idea (perhaps we want to say or plead, for example, that 'we are all equally animals'), but it is an idea that Derrida, like Diamond, clearly resists. In the iteralabile movement beyond the human, the idea of the difference is not only *not* effaced, it is affirmed. We are inclined to imagine that the idea of the difference would be most clearly in play where the path to an other is absolutely blocked; where our aliveness to the other animal simply gives out and we do not know what to say or do. But the thought of the iteralability of our responsiveness can encourage something else entirely. The idea of the difference does not show itself most radically or originally when a path to an other animal is closed, but in the ways in which, uncannily, *it is still found*. Along the multiple paths of our life with iteralabile marks, the human/animal difference, Derrida says, 'no longer forms a single indivisible line', but 'more than one internally divided line'.

'Be other than an animal', we say. The other demands something of me, the moral expectations I see in the gaze of the other who sees me, demand something of me – and that may not always be a human eye: 'Be other than an animal'. I am called (by the other, perhaps the other animal looking at me) to be human; called, then, to respect and not to diminish the alterity of every other.

And one is failing to respond to such a call to be human when one is beastly to the beast, beastly to the very one who can never be beastly.

So it is not that we form a non-biological concept of the human (via metaphysical insight or religious revelation or whatever) which can then be contrasted with the merely biological life of other living things. Nor are we to suppose that 'we are all equally animals'. Rather, the point is that *we have a non-biological concept of the animal too*. When we talk about animals, other creatures, the ones, for example, that we might see *seeing us*, we do not mean a being that is 'biologically an animal' or 'something with biological life' any more than our concept of the human means that. What we might call the 'fellow-creature response' involves the extension to animals of modes of thinking and acting that are especially characteristic of our responses to human beings – and so which belong most intimately to our concept of the human difference – and it does so in multiple and complex ways. Concepts of charity and justice are certainly involved here, as is the idea of the singularity of a life and concepts related to respect for that life – compassion, pity, gratitude and regret pointedly among them.

And yet, in a time when a life containing talk of the human difference seems more than ever content to violate the compassion and pity through which, in the name of that difference, we are called to find paths to animals, it is becoming increasingly difficult for that call to slip-across seem other than a merely sentimental slip-up. But the fact that a human being chooses his or her words as 'words from the heart', as Derrida does, and wants, for example, to mark *this cat's* unsubstitutable singularity, is not a mistake or error that stands in need of correction through a proper appreciation of a fundamentally unique 'truth of Man'. Nor need such words be spoken in naive ignorance of objective facts about, for example, an individual animal's membership of a genera, genus, or species. On the contrary, it simply goes to show how that *iteralabile* talk actually enters our lives, it shows us, as Diamond puts it, 'the shape – the "face" – that life containing such talk has'. It is, precisely, the 'face' of that life that is altered by what Derrida highlights as the '*unprecedented* proportions' of 'the subjection of the animal' that dominates modern life today. Indeed, as Wiggins notes, part of the unease that many feel about factory farming, intensive livestock rearing, the general spoliation of nature, and the extinction of innumerable animal species is that it shows us modern men and women, as in a mirror, as at certain points akin to a form of life we might well think 'profoundly alien': akin, that is, to an animal with 'no non-instrumental concerns and no interest in the world considered as lasting longer than the animal in question will need the world to last in order to sustain the animal's own life'. Such a life, we must not forget, is no preface to what remains to come *at all*.

Chapter 9
Starting over

I want to keep this concluding chapter short, very short, a very short conclusion to what has doubtless been a none too simple very short introduction to Derrida.

Jacques Derrida summed up his fears – and implied hopes – with regard to his readers in the following passage:

> Because I still like him, I can foresee the impatience of the bad reader: this is the way I name or accuse the fearful reader, the reader in a hurry to be determined, decided upon deciding (in order to annul, in other words to bring back to oneself, one has to wish to know in advance what to expect, one wishes to expect what has happened, one wishes to expect (oneself)). Now, it is *bad*, and I know of no other definition of the bad, it is bad to predestine one's reading, it is always bad to foretell. It is bad, reader, no longer to like retracing one's steps.

I am unbelievably grateful to the texts of Jacques Derrida for inciting me and continuing to incite me to retrace my steps, and to interrupt the readers I have been.

References

Chapter 1

Jacques Derrida, *Of Grammatology*, tr. G. Spivak (Baltimore: Johns Hopkins University Press, 1974).

Chapter 2

R. Morse and S. Collini (eds.), *The Cambridge Review*, Vol. 113, No. 2318 (Cambridge: Cambridge University Press, October 1992).

Barry Smith et al., 'Derrida Degree: A Question of Honour', *The Times*, Saturday, 9 May 1992.

Ludwig Wittgenstein, *Blue and Brown Books* (Oxford: Blackwell, 1958).

Jacques Derrida, in *Arguing with Derrida*, ed. Simon Glendinning (Oxford: Blackwell, 2001).

Edmund Husserl, 'Phenomenology and Anthropology', cited and translated by Robert Cumming in *Phenomenology and Deconstruction*, Vol. 3 (Chicago: Chicago University Press, 2001).

Bernard Williams, 'Contemporary Philosophy: A Second Look', in *The Blackwell Companion to Philosophy*, ed. N. Bunnin and E. Tsui-James (Oxford: Blackwell, 1996).

Gilbert Ryle, *The Concept of Mind* (Harmondsworth: Penguin, 1990).

H. Silverman and J. Barry (eds.), *Texts and Dialogues with Merleau-Ponty* (New York: Humanity Books, 1992).

Jacques Derrida, *Writing and Difference*, tr. A. Bass (London: Routledge, 1978).

Nicholas Royle, *Jacques Derrida* (London: Routledge, 2003). Derrida's observation that he was both 'excluded and favourite' occurs in his text 'Circumfession', which is published underneath Geoffrey Bennington's text 'Derridabase' in their joint publication *Jacques Derrida* (Chicago: Chicago University Press, 1993). In that text, Derrida tells of the death, 'a few months before I was conceived' of a brother he never knew, Paul Moïse, a brother who had been the youngest son before Jackie became, again, the youngest son. Jackie Derrida was the youngest son who took the place of the youngest son: 'from this I always got the feeling of being an excluded favourite, of both father and mother . . . excluded and favourite at two juxtaposed moments . . . and it is still going on, read the papers.'

Gavin Kitching, *Wittgenstein and Society* (Aldershot: Ashgate, 2003).

Ludwig Wittgenstein, *Philosophical Investigations*, tr. G. E. M. Anscombe (Oxford: Blackwell, 1958).

Jacques Derrida, *Of Grammatology*, tr. G. Spivak (Baltimore: Johns Hopkins University Press, 1974).

Chapter 3

There is a remarkable clip on *YouTube* in which Derrida discusses the 'truly exceptional moment' when the central ideas in *Of Grammatology* came to him, and evidently surprised him, in 1965. This should be related to the brief discussion of Derrida's 'virtuosity' at the end of this chapter. The link to the interview is http://www.youtube.com/watch?v=BSsDRf2wnOk, accessed 7 March 2011.

Jacques Derrida, *Of Grammatology*, tr. G. Spivak (Baltimore: Johns Hopkins University Press, 1974).

Jacques Derrida, *Ear of the Other*, tr. P. Kamuf (Lincoln: University of Nebraska Press, 1988).

Jacques Derrida, *A Taste for the Secret*, tr. G. Donis (Cambridge: Polity Press, 2001).

Roland Barthes, *S/Z*, tr. R. Miller (New York: Hill and Wang, 1974).

Hegel's plea to his readers not to 'take me seriously in a preface' since 'the real philosophical work is what I have just written' is cited by Gayatri Spivak in her 'Translator's Preface' to *Of Grammatology*.

Jacques Derrida, 'Outwork, prefacing', in *Dissemination*, tr. B. Johnson (London: Athlone Press, 1981).

Jacques Derrida, *The Politics of Friendship*, tr. G. Collins (London: Verso, 1997).

Jacques Derrida, *Rogues: Two Essays on Reason*, tr. P.-A. Brault and M. Naas (Stanford: Stanford University Press, 2004).

Jacques Derrida, *Points de suspension*(Paris: Galileé, 1997).

Chapter 4

Jacques Derrida, *Of Grammatology*, tr. G. Spivak (Baltimore: Johns Hopkins University Press, 1974).

Chapter 5

Jacques Derrida, 'White Mythology', in *Margins of Philosophy*, tr. A. Bass (London: Harvester Wheatsheaf, 1982).
Jacques Derrida, '"Eating Well", or the Calculation of the Subject', in *Who Comes After the Subject?*, ed. E. Cadava, P. Connor, and J.-L. Nancy (London: Routledge, 1991).
Jacques Derrida, 'Différance', in *Margins of Philosophy*, tr. A. Bass (London: Harvester Wheatsheaf, 1982).
Jacques Derrida, *Dissemination*, tr. B. Johnson (London: Athlone Press, 1981).

Chapter 6

Jacques Derrida, *Speech and Phenomena: And Other Essays on Husserl's Theory of Signs*, tr. D. B. Allison (Evanston: Northwestern University Press, 1973).
Geoffrey Bennington, *Legislations: The Politics of Deconstruction* (London: Verso, 1994).
Jacques Derrida, *Limited Inc*, ed. G. Graff, tr. S. Weber and J. Mehlman (Evanston: Northwestern University Press, 1988).
Jacques Derrida, *Positions*, tr. A. Bass (London: Athlone Press, 1987).
Geoffrey Bennington, *Interrupting Derrida* (London: Routledge, 2000).

Chapter 7

Jason Powell, *Jacques Derrida: A Biography* (London: Continuum, 2006).
Jacques Derrida, 'Force of Law: The "Mystical Foundation of Authority"', in *Deconstruction and the Possibility of Justice*, ed. D. Cornell, M. Rosenfeld, and D. Carlson (London: Routledge, 1992).
P. Goodrich, F. Hoffmann, M. Rosenfeld, and C. Vismann (eds.), *Derrida and Legal Philosophy* (London: Palgrave Macmillan, 2008).

Jacques Derrida, *Limited Inc*, ed. G. Graff, tr. S. Weber and J. Mehlman (Evanston: Northwestern University Press, 1988).

Jacques Derrida, *Of Grammatology*, tr. G. Spivak (Baltimore: Johns Hopkins University Press, 1974).

Jacques Derrida, in *Arguing with Derrida*, ed. S. Glendinning (Oxford: Blackwell, 2001).

Jacques Derrida, *Rogues: Two Essays on Reason*, tr. P.-A. Brault and M. Naas (Stanford: Stanford University Press, 2004).

Derrida's discussion of deconstruction and politics at Sussex University can be found at http://hydra.humanities.uci.edu/derrida/pol+fr.html, accessed 7 March 2011.

David Wiggins, 'Truth, Invention and the Meaning of Life', in *Needs, Values, Truth* (Oxford: Blackwell, 1987).

Jacques Derrida, *Specters of Marx*, tr. P. Kamuf (London: Routledge, 1994).

Jacques Derrida, *The Politics of Friendship*, tr. G. Collins (London: Verso, 1997).

Chapter 8

Martin Heidegger, *Being and Time*, tr. J. Macquarrie and E. Robinson (Oxford: Blackwell, 1962).

Jacques Derrida, *Of Grammatology*, tr. G. Spivak (Baltimore: Johns Hopkins University Press, 1974).

Jacques Derrida, in *Arguing with Derrida*, ed. S. Glendinning (Oxford: Blackwell, 2001).

Cora Diamond, 'Eating Meat and Eating People', in *The Realistic Spirit* (Cambridge, Mass.: MIT Press, 1996).

Cora Diamond, 'The Importance of Being Human', in *Human Beings*, ed. D. Cockburn (Cambridge: Cambridge University Press, 1991).

Jacques Derrida, 'The Animal That Therefore I Am (More to Follow)', tr. D. Wills, in *Critical Inquiry*, Vol. 29 (2002).

David Wiggins, 'Truth, Invention and the Meaning of Life', in *Needs, Values, Truth* (Oxford: Blackwell, 1987).

Chapter 9

Jacques Derrida, *The Post Card*, tr. A. Bass (Chicago: University of Chicago Press, 1987).

Further reading

Recommended works by Derrida in English

Speech and Phenomena: And Other Essays on Husserl's Theory of Signs, tr. D. B. Allison (Evanston: Northwestern University Press, 1973).

Of Grammatology, tr. G. Spivak (Baltimore: Johns Hopkins University Press, 1974).

Writing and Difference, tr. A. Bass (London: Routledge, 1978).

Dissemination, tr. B. Johnson (London: Athlone Press, 1981).

Margins of Philosophy, tr. A. Bass (Chicago: Chicago University Press, 1982).

'Geschlecht: Sexual Difference, Ontological Difference', tr. R. Berezdivin, *Research in Phenomenology*, 13 (1983).

Glas, tr. John P. Leavey, Jr., and R. Rand (Lincoln: University of Nebraska Press, 1986).

Positions, tr. A. Bass (London: Athlone Press, 1987).

The Post Card: From Socrates to Freud and Beyond, tr. A. Bass (Chicago: University of Chicago Press, 1987).

The Truth in Painting, tr. G. Bennington and I. McLeod (Chicago: Chicago University Press, 1987).

Limited Inc, ed. G. Graff, tr. S. Weber and J. Mehlman (Evanston: Northwestern University Press, 1988).

Of Spirit: Heidegger and the Question, tr. G. Bennington and R. Bowlby (Chicago: University of Chicago Press, 1989).

Acts of Literature, ed. Derek Attridge (London: Routledge, 1992).

The Other Heading: Reflections on Today's Europe, tr. P.-A. Brault and M. Naas (Bloomington: Indiana University Press, 1992).

Aporias, tr. T. Dutoit (Stanford: Stanford University Press, 1993).

Specters of Marx, tr. P. Kamuf (London: Routledge, 1994).
Points . . .: Interviews 1974–1994, tr. P. Kamuf and others (Stanford: Stanford University Press, 1995).
The Gift of Death, tr. D. Wills (Chicago: Chicago University Press, 1995).
Politics of Friendship, tr. G. Collins (London: Verso, 1997).
'Faith and Knowledge', tr. S. Weber, in *Religion*, ed. J. Derrida and G. Vattimo (Cambridge: Polity Press, 1998).
Monolingualism of the Other; or, The Prosthesis of Origin, tr. P. Mensah (Stanford: Stanford University Press, 1998).
Of Hospitality, tr. R. Bowlby (Stanford: Stanford University Press, 2000).
'I Have a Taste for the Secret', in *A Taste for the Secret*, ed. J. Derrida and M. Ferraris (Cambridge: Polity Press, 2001).
On Cosmopolitanism and Forgiveness, tr. M. Dooley and M. Hughes (London: Routledge, 2001).
Negotiations: Interventions and Interviews, 1971–2001, tr. E. Rottenberg (Stanford: Stanford University Press, 2002).
Without Alibi, ed. and tr. P. Kamuf (Stanford: Stanford University Press, 2002).
Who's Afraid of Philosophy?: Right to Philosophy 1, tr. J. Plug (Stanford: Stanford University Press, 2002).
'The Animal That Therefore I Am (More to Follow)', tr. D. Wills, in *Critical Inquiry*, Vol. 29 (2002).
Philosophy in a Time of Terror: Dialogues with Jürgen Habermas and Jacques Derrida, ed. G. Borradori (Chicago: University of Chicago Press, 2003).
Rogues: Two Essays on Reason, tr. P.-A. Brault and M. Naas (Stanford: Stanford University Press, 2004).
Learning to Live Finally: The Last Interview, with Jean Birnbaum, tr. P.-A. Brault and M. Naas (Hoboken, NJ: Melville House, 2007).
The Beast and the Sovereign, Vol. I, tr. G. Bennington (Chicago: University of Chicago Press, 2009).

Recommended works on Derrida in English

Geoffrey Bennington, *Legislations: The Politics of Deconstruction* (London: Verso, 1994).
Geoffrey Bennington, *Interrupting Derrida* (London: Routledge, 2000).
Geoffrey Bennington, *Not Half No End: Militantly Melancholic Essays in Memory of Jacques Derrida* (Edinburgh: Edinburgh University Press, 2010).

Hélène Cixous, 'Jacques Derrida as a Proteus Unbound', tr. P. Kamuf, in *Critical Inquiry*, 33 (Winter 2007).
Robert Denoon Cumming, *Phenomenology and Deconstruction*, 4 vols. (Chicago: Chicago University Press, 1991–2001).
Simon Glendinning and Robert Eaglestone (eds.), *Derrida's Legacies: Literature and Philosophy* (Abingdon: Routledge, 2008).
Martin Hägglund, *Radical Atheism: Derrida and the Time of Life* (Stanford: Stanford University Press, 2008).
Marian Hobson, *Jacques Derrida: Opening Lines* (London: Routledge, 1998).
Christopher Johnson, *Derrida: The Scene of Writing* (London: Phoenix Press, 1997).
Peggy Kamuf, *To Follow: The Wake of Jacques Derrida* (Edinburgh: Edinburgh University Press, 2010).
Martin McQuillan, *Deconstruction after 9/11* (Abingdon: Routledge, 2009).
Michael Naas, *Derrida From Now On* (New York: Fordham University Press, 2008).
Christopher Norris, *Deconstruction: Theory and Practice* (London: Methuen, 1982).
Jack Reynolds and James Roffe (eds.), *Understanding Derrida* (London: Continuum, 2004).
Nicholas Royle, *Jacques Derrida* (London: Routledge, 2003).
Nicholas Royle, *In Memory of Jacques Derrida* (Edinburgh: Edinburgh University Press, 2009).
Gayatri Chakravorty Spivak, 'Translator's Preface', in Jacques Derrida, *Of Grammatology* (Baltimore: Johns Hopkins University Press, 1974).
Sarah Wood, *Derrida's Writing and Difference: A Reader's Guide* (London: Continuum, 2009).

Index

A

B

C

D

L

M

N

O

P

Q

R

S

T

U

W

Z

Expand your collection of VERY SHORT INTRODUCTIONS

1. Classics
2. Music
3. Buddhism
4. Literary Theory
5. Hinduism
6. Psychology
7. Islam
8. Politics
9. Theology
10. Archaeology
11. Judaism
12. Sociology
13. The Koran
14. The Bible
15. Social and Cultural Anthropology
16. History
17. Roman Britain
18. The Anglo-Saxon Age
19. Medieval Britain
20. The Tudors
21. Stuart Britain
22. Eighteenth-Century Britain
23. Nineteenth-Century Britain
24. Twentieth-Century Britain
25. Heidegger
26. Ancient Philosophy
27. Socrates
28. Marx
29. Logic
30. Descartes
31. Machiavelli
32. Aristotle
33. Hume
34. Nietzsche
35. Darwin
36. The European Union
37. Gandhi
38. Augustine
39. Intelligence
40. Jung
41. Buddha
42. Paul
43. Continental Philosophy
44. Galileo
45. Freud
46. Wittgenstein
47. Indian Philosophy
48. Rousseau
49. Hegel
50. Kant
51. Cosmology
52. Drugs
53. Russian Literature
54. The French Revolution
55. Philosophy
56. Barthes
57. Animal Rights
58. Kierkegaard
59. Russell
60. Shakespeare
61. Clausewitz
62. Schopenhauer
63. The Russian Revolution

64. Hobbes
65. World Music
66. Mathematics
67. Philosophy of Science
68. Cryptography
69. Quantum Theory
70. Spinoza
71. Choice Theory
72. Architecture
73. Poststructuralism
74. Postmodernism
75. Democracy
76. Empire
77. Fascism
78. Terrorism
79. Plato
80. Ethics
81. Emotion
82. Northern Ireland
83. Art Theory
84. Locke
85. Modern Ireland
86. Globalization
87. The Cold War
88. The History of Astronomy
89. Schizophrenia
90. The Earth
91. Engels
92. British Politics
93. Linguistics
94. The Celts
95. Ideology
96. Prehistory
97. Political Philosophy
98. Postcolonialism
99. Atheism
100. Evolution
101. Molecules
102. Art History
103. Presocratic Philosophy
104. The Elements
105. Dada and Surrealism
106. Egyptian Myth
107. Christian Art
108. Capitalism
109. Particle Physics
110. Free Will
111. Myth
112. Ancient Egypt
113. Hieroglyphs
114. Medical Ethics
115. Kafka
116. Anarchism
117. Ancient Warfare
118. Global Warming
119. Christianity
120. Modern Art
121. Consciousness
122. Foucault
123. The Spanish Civil War
124. The Marquis de Sade
125. Habermas
126. Socialism
127. Dreaming
128. Dinosaurs
129. Renaissance Art
130. Buddhist Ethics
131. Tragedy
132. Sikhism
133. The History of Time
134. Nationalism
135. The World Trade Organization

136. Design
137. The Vikings
138. Fossils
139. Journalism
140. The Crusades
141. Feminism
142. Human Evolution
143. The Dead Sea Scrolls
144. The Brain
145. Global Catastrophes
146. Contemporary Art
147. Philosophy of Law
148. The Renaissance
149. Anglicanism
150. The Roman Empire
151. Photography
152. Psychiatry
153. Existentialism
154. The First World War
155. Fundamentalism
156. Economics
157. International Migration
158. Newton
159. Chaos
160. African History
161. Racism
162. Kabbalah
163. Human Rights
164. International Relations
165. The American Presidency
166. The Great Depression and The New Deal
167. Classical Mythology
168. The New Testament as Literature
169. American Political Parties and Elections
170. Bestsellers
171. Geopolitics
172. Antisemitism
173. Game Theory
174. HIV/AIDS
175. Documentary Film
176. Modern China
177. The Quakers
178. German Literature
179. Nuclear Weapons
180. Law
181. The Old Testament
182. Galaxies
183. Mormonism
184. Religion in America
185. Geography
186. The Meaning of Life
187. Sexuality
188. Nelson Mandela
189. Science and Religion
190. Relativity
191. The History of Medicine
192. Citizenship
193. The History of Life
194. Memory
195. Autism
196. Statistics
197. Scotland
198. Catholicism
199. The United Nations
200. Free Speech
201. The Apocryphal Gospels
202. Modern Japan
203. Lincoln
204. Superconductivity
205. Nothing
206. Biography

207. The Soviet Union
208. Writing and Script
209. Communism
210. Fashion
211. Forensic Science
212. Puritanism
213. The Reformation
214. Thomas Aquinas
215. Deserts
216. The Norman Conquest
217. Biblical Archaeology
218. The Reagan Revolution
219. The Book of Mormon
220. Islamic History
221. Privacy
222. Neoliberalism
223. Progressivism
224. Epidemiology
225. Information
226. The Laws of Thermodynamics
227. Innovation
228. Witchcraft
229. The New Testament
230. French Literature
231. Film Music
232. Druids
233. German Philosophy
234. Advertising
235. Forensic Psychology
236. Modernism
237. Leadership
238. Christian Ethics
239. Tocqueville
240. Landscapes and Geomorphology
241. Spanish Literature
242. Diplomacy
243. North American Indians
244. The U.S. Congress
245. Romanticism
246. Utopianism
247. The Blues
248. Keynes
249. English Literature
250. Agnosticism
251. Aristocracy
252. Martin Luther
253. Michael Faraday
254. Planets
255. Pentecostalism
256. Humanism
257. Folk Music
258. Late Antiquity
259. Genius
260. Numbers
261. Muhammad
262. Beauty
263. Critical Theory
264. Organizations
265. Early Music
266. The Scientific Revolution
267. Cancer
268. Nuclear Power
269. Paganism
270. Risk
271. Science Fiction
272. Herodotus
273. Conscience
274. American Immigration
275. Jesus
276. Viruses
277. Protestantism
278. Derrida

PHILOSOPHY

A Very Short Introduction

Edward Craig

This lively and engaging book is the ideal introduction for anyone who has ever been puzzled by what philosophy is or what it is for.

Edward Craig argues that philosophy is not an activity from another planet: learning about it is just a matter of broadening and deepening what most of us do already. He shows that philosophy is no mere intellectual pastime: thinkers such as Plato, Buddhist writers, Descartes, Hobbes, Hume, Hegel, Darwin, Mill and de Beauvoir were responding to real needs and events – much of their work shapes our lives today, and many of their concerns are still ours.

> 'A vigorous and engaging introduction that speaks to the philosopher in everyone.'
>
> **John Cottingham, University of Reading**

> 'addresses many of the central philosophical questions in an engaging and thought-provoking style . . . Edward Craig is already famous as the editor of the best long work on philosophy (the Routledge Encyclopedia); now he deserves to become even better known as the author of one of the best short ones.'
>
> **Nigel Warburton, The Open University**

www.oup.com/vsi

CONTINENTAL PHILOSOPHY

A Very Short Introduction

Simon Critchley

Continental philosophy is a contested concept which cuts to the heart of the identity of philosophy and its relevance to matters of public concern and personal life. This book attempts to answer the question 'What is Continental philosophy?' by telling a story that began with Kant 200 years ago and includes discussions of major philosophers like Nietzsche, Husserl and Heidegger. At the core of the book is a plea to place philosophy at the centre of cultural life, and thus reawaken its ancient definition of the love of wisdom that makes life worth living.

> 'Antagonism and mutual misrepresentation between so-called analytical and continental philosophy have helped shape the course of every significant development in Western intellectual life since the 1960s – structuralism, post-structuralism, postmodernism, gender studies, etc. Simon Critchley has skilfully and sympathetically sketched continental lines of thought so that strangers to their detail may enter them systematically enough that their principle texts begin to illuminate one another. It is a remarkable achievement.'
>
> **Stanley Cavell, Harvard University**

www.oup.com/vsi